THE
WOMEN
OF
AZUA

Older woman in backyard thatch-roofed kitchen.
Cooking is done on the charcoal burners at left.

THE
WOMEN
OF
AZUA

Work and Family
in the Rural Dominican Republic

Barbara Finlay

New York
Westport, Connecticut
London

Library of Congress Cataloging-in-Publication Data

Finlay, Barbara.
    The women of Azua : work and family in the rural Dominican
Republic / Barbara Finlay.
        p.   cm.
    Bibliography: p.
    Includes index.
    ISBN 0-275-93220-6 (alk. paper)
    1. Women agricultural workers—Dominican Republic—Azua (Province)
2. Women in rural development—Dominican Republic—Azua (Province)
3. Rural families—Dominican Republic—Azua (Province)   4. Family
life surveys—Dominican Republic—Azua (Province)   5. Agricultural
processing industries—Dominican Republic—Azua (Province)   6. Azua
(Dominican Republic : Province)—Rural conditions.
    HD6073.A292D654   1989
    331.4'83'09729372—dc20   89-35842

Library of Congress Catalog Card Number: 89-35842
ISBN: 0-275-93220-6

First published in 1989

Praeger Publishers, One Madison Avenue, New York, NY 10010
A division of Greenwood Press, Inc.

Printed in the United States of America

The paper used in this book complies with the Permanent
Paper Standard issued by the National Information Standards
Organization (Z39.48-1984).

10 9 8 7 6 5 4 3 2 1

For my children,

Ginger, Kerry, and Michael

Contents

Tables

Preface

A book such as this is the culmination of a long process of planning, research, analysis, writing, and revision. Without the assistance of a great number of people, it would not have reached this point. I would therefore like to take this opportunity to acknowledge the contributions of some of the more important collaborators in this effort.

First, to the interviewers, without whose work this research would never have been done, I owe a great debt. They are Magdalena Reyes, Alba Nurys Beltre, Nandina Pina, Amancia de los Santos, Dulce de los Santos, Eunice Oviedo, Eridania Santana, Bethania Silvestre, Rosalia Ferreras, Raquel Valenzuela, Thelma A. C. Marcelo, Melania Feliz, Belkis Arias, and Olga de los Santos. These young women worked quickly and willingly, without complaint. I could not have hoped for a more competent or enthusiastic group of research assistants. When I left them for the last time, I felt as if I were leaving old friends.

Fausto Alvarez, a Dominican who was at the time a master's candidate in sociology at Texas A&M, served for a summer as research associate. It was he who trained the interviewers and helped with much of the logistics of carrying out the survey. His work was invaluable and contributed greatly to the high quality of the work done by the interviewers.

I should also like to acknowledge the great help given at the outset of this project by two sociologists who were working for a water-use project in Azua--Bernard DeLaine and Alberto Mejia. They took time out of their busy schedules, helped introduce us to the area, and located the women who became our interviewers. They provided much support and advice throughout the project.

Others who should be thanked are Eulalia Jimenez and her colleagues at the Santo Domingo office of Mujeres en Desarrollo Dominicana (MUDE), who provided information about rural women of the country. Much of the first draft of this book was written while I was a Fulbright scholar working in the Instituto Central de Investigaciones, Universidad Nacional Pedro Henriquez Urena, Santo Domingo. The director, Julio-Cesar Mejia, provided much material and moral support during the academic year, for which I am grateful. Also very supportive were the rector, Dr. Jaime Vinas Roman, and the vice rector, Mr. Francisco Polanco.

I had research support from a number of sources First, from the College of Liberal Arts of Texas A&M University, which awarded me a summer research grant that allowed me to get started and seek out other funds. The USAID-Santo Domingo Women in Development officer, Debra McFarland, was instrumental in obtaining funding from that agency for the major portion of research expenses. The Council for International Exchange of Scholars, which administers the Fulbright program, was also an important contributor to this project, since it was the Fulbright award that allowed me to remain in the Dominican Republic for a full year, enriching my understanding of the culture and the status of women there. Of particular help in easing my way through the residency there were Janice Byrd of Council for the International Exchange of Scholars in Washington, and Lezetta Moyer, cultural attache for the U.S. Embassy in Santo Domingo.

Jackie Sandles typed and retyped the manuscript with patience and skill, and her enthusiasm for the work was always gratifying.

Finally, I wish to thank the women of the Azua communities who took time from their daily labors to be interviewed, contributing the heart of this book. My admiration and respect for these women was deepened as a result of getting to know them during the study. I hope that I, for my part, have produced a manuscript that depicts them fairly and truthfully, and that it is worthy of all of the fine efforts of everyone who contributed to the project.

1   Introduction

This book is based on field observations and a survey of women in six rural communities in the southwestern Dominican Republic. The general purpose of the study was to assess the impact of the women's employment at large agricultural companies on various aspects of their lives: their status within their communities, their status within their families, their attitudes, and their hopes for the future. In addition, this study provides basic data about women in a setting never before studied by North American sociologists. In this introductory chapter, the basic goals and reasons for the study are described.

WOMEN AND DEVELOPMENT

There has been increasing interest in the past few years in the roles of women in traditional agricultural systems and in the effects of economic development on women and families. (See, for example, Boserup 1970; Nash and Safa 1986; Massiah 1983; and Leacock, Safa, and Contributors 1986.) In the past, not much attention was paid to such matters, either by scholars or by development planners. Many projects were planned and carried out with the assumption that those projects which help men would automatically help women, since (presumably) women were maintained by their husbands and/or fathers, and since women were not "economically active" or "productive." Thus, any improvement in men's income and status was bound to benefit women as well.

The tendency to ignore women when thinking of economic development or activity is well illustrated by a conversation I had when I first arrived in Santo Domingo in the spring of 1986. I was there on a two-week preparatory trip before the beginning of my year-long residence. During that visit, I went from agency to agency, trying to get background information for my study and to make preliminary contacts and arrangements. One of my visits was to the Direccion Nacional de Estadisticas (National Statistics Office, the equivalent of the U.S. Census Bureau), where I met with a very high official of that agency. I had not yet decided exactly where I would do my study, but the Azua area was emerging as a strong probability the more I learned of its recent economic development. I asked the official what he could tell me about the area of Azua. Smiling with pride, the official told me, "In Azua, there is no unemployment." This pronouncement by so high an official of the national statistical office both surprised and puzzled me. It surprised me because I knew that unemployment in general was very high in the rural Dominican Republic. It puzzled me because I could not believe that a man in his position would be totally mistaken about such a statistic--though obviously he had to be exaggerating. I began to think that the many investments in the Azua area that I had heard of had really had a major impact on levels of employment there. This would indeed be an interesting area to study!

Later, after leaving that office with copies of census publications and survey reports about demographic and economic characteristics of the Dominican Republic, I was able to check the validity of the official's statement with his own office's data. What I found was very interesting and revealing. According to official statistics, it is true that unemployment in Azua is low--for men. In the rural zone, the male unemployment rate was lower than in any other region of the country, about 10 percent. So, although the claim of "no unemployment" was an exaggeration, it had some basis in fact.

However, in the same data were statistics for the women of the rural zones in Azua. Those unemployment rates were the *highest* among all regions in the country: fully 63 percent of the rural women in the Azua region were classified as unemployed, according to the labor survey data (ONE 1980). This statistic does not mean that 63 percent of women were not working--that percentage is higher--but that

63 percent of those women defined as economically active (those who had been employed or who would like to be employed if they had the opportunity) were not employed. Obviously, for the official of the National Statistics Office, employment/unemployment refers to men's activities only. Women's unemployment does not enter into his estimation of the economic well-being of a community.

I repeat this anecdote not to embarrass or accuse the particular official or his office, but because his attitude is so typical of the attitudes of development planners, bureaucrats, and investors. The assumption is repeatedly made that projects that help and employ men will automatically help women and children as well. Thus, women's economic activities are simply ignored, being considered irrelevant to the real problems of economic development.

Unfortunately, the real world is not so simple. There are many reasons why a lack of attention to women can produce problems in the development process. One of the most important is that, in all regions of the world, including less developed areas, the percentage of families headed and supported by women alone is increasing. More and more women have to be "economically active" in order to support themselves and their children. And in every country, these women tend to be heavily concentrated among the poorest families (Massiah 1983). The problems of unemployment, poverty, and sex discrimination fall heavily on these women.

A second reason for considering women in the development process is that the development of skills, technology, and employment for men does not always bring beneficial results for the women in their families. Such projects can cause changes in the traditional balance of resources and/or power within the family, often leaving the women more dependent than ever on their husbands. It may also deprive them of formerly meaningful and productive economic roles. For example, Massiah writes, "The modernization process of Caribbean economies, with its highly visible focus on imported technology, specialized enterprises, and individualistic philosophy, has served to undercut women in the one area [that is, fruit and vegetable marketing] in which they had gained predominance" (1983:57). The development process can also lead to conflicts within families and higher divorce or desertion rates, thus leaving women relatively worse off economically (Safa 1986).

In addition, in many cultures, the income of a man is defined as "his," and is not necessarily expected to be pooled with other "family income", nor even necessarily spent on basic needs of the family. Expenses for food, health, education, and clothes may be considered to be the responsibility of women, to be paid for by their income. If wives have no income, they must ask husbands for whatever money they need; the husbands control the amount they receive. Husbands in such situations are free to spend their money on purely personal pursuits that do not help the woman or the family. In this situation, the woman depends on the goodwill of the husband, and she has little recourse if he is not willing to share with her the benefits of his increased income from male-oriented development projects. To quote the 1982 USAID policy paper *Women in Development*, the "predominant misperception about disposition of income within poor families . . . has given rise to critical miscalculations in project planning" (USAID 1982:3).

Finally, projects that provide opportunities for men but none for women are increasingly criticized for their unfairness to women. People in all regions of the world are coming to believe that women, as well as men, should have options in their lives and should have the opportunity to develop their talents, to have their productive activities recognized, and to have access to training, resources, and employment (see, for example, Morgan 1984).

Thus, for these and other reasons, there is an increased interest in projects that include women as recipients of training, aid, or other benefits, as well as in studies of the impacts of various types of projects on women and families. In addition, there is a need for basic studies of the "gender-related dynamics of decision-making, resource allocation, and financial responsibility within the household" among target groups for development (USAID 1982:4). The study that is the basis of this book was undertaken for these purposes: to understand the traditional division of labor and decision making within households, and to see the changes that occur when women move from traditional roles into the market economy as wage earners. This study focuses on a specific type of employment, work for large agribusiness companies, usually multinational and export-oriented. This is of interest because of the growing number of private companies that are locating production units in Third World countries, often providing employment opportunities for women.

EXPORT-PROCESSING INDUSTRIES AND WOMEN

Since the 1960s there has been a rapid increase in the placement of export-processing industries in Third World countries, where production of goods for marketing in the United States or other highly industrialized countries takes place. The primary reason behind this new form of multinational corporate activity is the availability of cheap labor, along with weak or nonexistent unionization and cheap resources. This represents a "new international division of labor," in which underdeveloped countries are becoming sites for manufacturing instead of primarily suppliers of raw materials for production in other countries (Froebel et al 1978:23; Nash and Fernandez-Kelly 1983). Most of this type of investment takes place in countries with "low wages, high unemployment, limited natural resources, and politically stable regimes" (Safa 1986:58). The governments of these countries often encourage this type of development by providing such incentives as tax breaks, subsidized credit, and freedom from import duties on machinery necessary for the enterprise. In turn, the developing countries hope to improve their foreign-exchange earnings, to reduce unemployment with the jobs created by the industries, to increase the level of skills of workers, and to transfer advanced technology into the host country (Safa 1986; Froebel et al 1978). In fact, most of these goals are not usually attained by the underdeveloped country (Froebel et al 1978).

In many of these industries, the great majority of workers recruited are women, a "radical departure from the pattern of most multi-nationals," which formerly had hired mainly men in highly mechanized and capital-intensive operations (Safa 1986:59).

> The employment structure in export production is [unbalanced.] ... The criteria are lowest wage cost and highest performance and productivity, using unskilled and semi-skilled labor. As a result, predominantly women in the younger age groups are employed. (Froebel et al 1978:25)

One type of export-oriented industry that has become increasingly common in recent decades is that of food production for export. Tomatoes, melons, strawberries, beef, and many other food products are grown in less developed countries under the auspices of large companies such as Del Monte, Castle and Cook, and United Brands. These foods are harvested, processed, and packed for shipment to developed countries, where they are sold at a much higher profit than would be possible if they had been grown in the more developed country. The advantage to the company is the ready availability of cheap labor, as well as cheap land and favorable concessions from the governments of the less developed countries (Arizpe and Aranda 1981; Safa 1986).

Many studies have pointed out the "macroeconomic effects" of this type of development on the country in which it is situated (see, for example, Froebel et al 1978). However, few have studied its more micro-level impacts. Referring to export-processing industries in general, Safa (1986:59) writes, "few [studies] have given attention to the type of labor recruited, other than to characterize it as cheap and unskilled." Among the questions that Safa raises concerning the effects of export processing industries on the women who become their employees are the following: Are the new possibilities for employment improving their status in society? What effect has export processing had on the traditional division of labor by sex and, in particular, on family structure? These questions are an important aspect of the present study. In order to put them in context, we must first consider the general process by which women have been "marginalized" (Tiano 1987) by the capitalist development process.

CAPITALISM AND MARGINALIZATION

In many precapitalist cultures, women and men in the family were interdependent, so that neither could survive without the other. Men carried out some productive activities, perhaps plowing, harvesting, and trading. Women carried out other necessary activities, usually including food and clothing production, animal care, and some work in the fields. The particular sets of activities done by men and by women varied greatly--in many "slash and burn" cultures, for example, men cleared the forests while women planted and tended the crops (Lenski 1966). But whatever the specific division of labor, in most cases neither men nor women could get along without the work of the other.

With the coming of the capitalist market and wage labor, the traditional balance between men and women was upset. As Western models of "work" were imposed upon underdeveloped nations, men were given skills and resources to produce a marketable crop or product, while women were ignored, on the assumption that they would be "taken care of" by the men in their families. Women's traditional work was devalued because it did not yield a marketable product. And with "development" came the inevitable inflation of prices. Thus women were left out of a system that increasingly demanded cash but offered the possibility of earning cash to men only.

Women thus became more dependent on men, and this dependence was exacerbated by the traditional patriarchal cultural beliefs, which condone discrimination against women in the formal labor market and unequal treatment in the family. Yet, while in this system women depend on men to support them, men are no longer dependent on women's productive work to survive. Indeed, a man may be "better off" spending his income on himself and not giving it to his family. Or he may choose to share it with a woman who is not his wife. The point is that wage labor does not support family stability as traditional agriculture did. Women are now both more dependent and more vulnerable to loss of support than ever before (Boserup 1970; Lim 1983; Tiano 1987; Arizpe and Aranda 1981).

Everywhere women have reacted to this process of marginalization by moving into the labor market, although with great disadvantages. They have tended to move into the informal sector in jobs seen as extensions of their traditional roles (e.g., sellers of fried foods), or they have become domestic servants or prostitutes (Tiano 1987). The employment of women in export processing plants needs to be seen in this context. Women are hired by these companies precisely because they are marginalized by the development process. They thus can be hired at low wages, for long hours, and under poor working conditions. It is therefore unrealistic to believe that this employment represents a step up the ladder of social mobility. These are dead-end jobs at the lowest level of the wage structure. Women accept them gladly because they have few alternatives in a system that is structured to favor men (Lim 1983; Tiano 1987; Fernandez-Kelly 1983; Arizpe and Aranda 1981).

Yet, as Lim (1983) points out, such employment can have some important effects at the local level, in terms of breaking down traditional patriarchal definitions of women's proper roles in the home. But, she argues, it "cannot significantly undermine the patriarchal social relations responsible for women's inferior labor market position on which their very employment is predicated" (Lim 1983:84).

The effect of employment on these women's status in the community and within the family, according to previous studies, is often very limited because of the low wages, the often temporary nature of the job, and the high turnover rates (Safa 1986). The job may give the women a bit of independence in the home, as long as it lasts, but they usually work under very unfavorable conditions, with low wages, lack of job security, no opportunity for advancement, and often unhealthy and unsafe job environments (Arizpe and Aranda 1981;Lim 1983; Safa 1986).

GOALS OF THIS STUDY

In the present study, women in a few small rural communities near several large agribusiness food production facilities are studied. Most of what these companies raise is for export, the main crops being melons and tomatoes, although some large-scale operations also exist for domestic consumption. The setting is in the southern Dominican Republic, a country that has a strong patriarchal tradition as well as high unemployment. In this study, we will not deal with the macro-level questions concerning the economic impacts of these companies on the community or the country. Our goals are to try to assess some of the impacts of these companies, through their employment of women, on the families, attitudes, level of living, and aspirations of the women themselves. This is done through a survey of two groups of women: a representative sample of the women of the communities (the "community sample") and a special sample of women employees of these companies (the "worker sample").

In addition, this study provides descriptive data about the general social characteristics of women in small rural communities in the Dominican Republic. Up to now, there have been very few empirically based studies of women or of the family in this country, so data from this study will provide useful information on these subjects. (See Cross-Beras 1980 for a discussion of the need for this type of study.)

The major goals of this study, then, are (1) to describe the social characteristics of the rural women in one area of the Dominican Republic and (2) to measure the impact of industrial employment on women and their families. Among the specific research questions to be addressed by the research are these:

1. What type of women are employed by the companies? How do they differ from the other women of the community on such characteristics as age, education, age at marriage, number of years in the community, and migration history?

2. What impacts can be seen on various aspects of the workers' lives and families? Do they differ substantially from the other women of their communities in level of living, marital status and history, and fertility? Do they differ in attitudes about marriage and children, contraception, and women's roles? Do they have different aspirations for their children? Do they have more power and resources within the family?

We might expect, for example, that workers would be more independent and less traditional in their attitudes and behaviors within the family, and that they would have higher aspirations for their sons and (especially) daughters, compared with the general population of women in these communities. We will look at such characteristics as levels of living, employment and resources, marital status and attitudes, resource division, decision making, division of labor in the household, nutrition and health, contraception, childbearing, and aspirations for children. For each topic, a comparison is made between the representative sample of women of the communities studied and the sample of women workers. From the community sample data, we will learn more about the typical woman in the rural southwestern Dominican Republic. The worker sample will help us to see how a woman's life is different because of her work for an export food processing company.

2 Geographical and Historical Setting

The Dominican Republic is relatively unknown to most people in the United States, even though it lies less than three hours by plane from Miami. As a matter of fact, the Dominican capital of Santo Domingo is closer to Miami than is Houston, Texas, Washington, D.C., or Nashville, Tennessee.

This small country is located on the island of Hispaniola, second largest of the Caribbean islands. The Dominican Republic occupies the eastern two-thirds of the island, with Haiti making up the remaining third. The island lies between Cuba to the west and Puerto Rico to the east, both of which receive much more attention in the U.S. press than their neighbors in between.

Those Americans who are aware of the Dominican Republic usually know it as a sunny tourist destination with beautiful beaches, golf, tennis, casinos, and *merengue* music. In addition, many North Americans recall the brief 1965 U.S. Marine invasion ordered by President Johnson, although few have any understanding of what led to the U.S. involvement. And to older Americans, the name Trujillo still has a familiar ring. However, few people in this country are aware of the real people, the customs, the history, or the politics of the Dominican Republic, even though it has many ties to the United States. Today it is an important trading partner of the United States, the site of a growing number of North American business ventures, and a contributor of more Hispanic migrants to the United States than any other Latin American country except Mexico.

There are a number of English-language books about the Dominican Republic. However, these studies are almost all devoted to political history, mostly focusing on the Trujillo dictatorship, the civil strife and U.S. involvement in the 1960s, and the subsequent economic dependency on the United States (see, for example, Bell 1981; Feinberg 1984; Lowenthal 1972; Wiarda and Kryzanek 1982).

Especially neglected have been the family, rural communities, and women. What little has been written on these topics has generally been lacking in empirical foundation, biased toward the upper and middle classes, and often based on stereotypical notions rather than reality (see Cross-Beras 1980; Weil 1973.) One important goal of this book is to address this gap in the literature by looking at the everyday lives of women and families in some small rural Dominican communities.

BRIEF HISTORICAL OVERVIEW

It was on the island of Hispaniola that Christopher Columbus first set foot on American soil in December 1492, naming it and claiming it for the Spanish crown. The city of Santo Domingo, founded in 1496, is the oldest in the Americas. In the succeeding 400 years, the island has had a history of violence, conquest, and political upheaval, having been at various times under Spanish, French, English, and Haitian rule. The eastern part finally established independence in 1844, but with continuing instability and repression (Geggus 1982:6-23; Heinl and Heinl 1978:10-24; Knight 1970:1-5).

Beginning in 1510, the Spanish crown had authorized the importation of 4,000 African slaves per year for use in mining and later in the cultivation of sugarcane. According to Leyburn (1966:18), the black slave population in the eighteenth century had reached over 450,000, greatly outnumbering the 68,000 whites and freedmen.

Demographically and culturally, the Dominican Republic appears to be largely a product of these Afro-Spanish roots, the indigenous peoples having been wiped out by European-borne diseases, slave exploitation, and outright genocide (Fiske 1899; Heinl and Heinl 1978:13; Weddle 1974:16). Non-Spanish Europeans were never numerous on the eastern side of the island. The current population consists mainly of "mixed" descendants of the original Spanish and African populations, with Spanish spoken by all.

In the late nineteenth and early twentieth centuries, the Dominican Republic came increasingly under the influence and domination of the United States. Though formally recognizing the smaller country's independence, the United States has, at various times since 1844, invaded the country, controlled its elections, threatened its leaders, exercised economic pressure, and even tried to annex it for its economic resources. American troops occupied the Dominican Republic from 1916 to 1924, during which time American economic activity greatly increased, to the detriment of the domestic economy (Knight 1970:34; Alvarez 1988:31-33).

Quickly following the early occupation came 30 years of repressive domination of the country by Rafael Trujillo, established and maintained largely through his rigid control of the military and his carefully groomed reputation in the United States as a defender against "communism" (Gleijeses 1978:23). After Trujillo's assassination in 1961 and following the subsequent election of the progressive Juan Bosch as the new president, the U.S. invasion took place in 1965 (actually the second time that U.S. Marines had been sent into the country), as President Johnson sought to establish a more "friendly" government. The U.S. intervention led to the election of Joaquin Balaguer as the U.S.-approved president in 1966. Balaguer, a former Trujillo protege, was described by Gleijeses (1973:300) as "murderous and oppressive," but his policies were approved by Washington because of their perceived pro-U.S. consequences. In 1978, the more reformist and progressive *Partido Revolucionario Dominicano* (PRD) won the presidency, and during the two successive administrations of Antonio Guzman and Salvador Jorge-Blanco, the country's civil liberties and institutional development greatly improved. In May 1986, Joaquin Balaguer was reelected president, following revelations of extreme corruption within the Jorge-Blanco government; his second presidency has apparently been much less repressive and somewhat more politically independent of U.S. influence than the first.

Still, the Dominican Republic suffers, as do most Latin American countries, from increasing dependence on political and economic players external to the country and its control. Of particular importance and relevance to the present study are increasing inflation, devaluation of the currency, and exploitation of the country's low wage/low regulation climate by multinational companies. All of these factors have led to an increase in paid labor by women, and hence to the subject of this study.

Today's Dominican Republic has an area of 18,700 square miles, with 870 miles of coastline and 193 miles of border with Haiti. Its 1981 population was 5,647,977, and current estimates are near 7,000,000 (Paxton 1987).

THE SOUTHWESTERN REGION AND AZUA

The study that forms the basis of this book was carried out in eight small rural communities near the city of Azua, which lies in the southwestern Dominican Republic. The city of Azua is some 120 kilometers west of Santo Domingo. The Azua Valley is located between two mountain ranges, the Sierra Martin Garcia and the Central Cordillera. The region has a semiarid climate, with an average temperature in the high 80s (Farenheit) and an average annual rainfall of 373 mm. From May through July and September through November, rainfall is heaviest, the drier months being December, January, and February. Because of the summer heat, there is heavy water loss to evaporation, especially in July and August.

The traveler west along Highway 2 from Santo Domingo to Azua sees people everywhere along the road. The terrain is hilly, and planted with fields of sugarcane, tomatoes, and corn. There may be several wagons loaded (or being loaded) with cane (*caña*), pulled by teams of oxen. There are always many trucks and small buses on the road, carrying wares to and from Santo Domingo. Along the roadside every few miles there are fruit or vegetable vendors sitting behind neat stacks of mangoes, tomatoes, or whatever is in season, waiting for passersby to stop and buy.

There are also likely to be many people on motorcycles or scooters, a cheap and fast way to travel. Some of these are "commercial" transportation, taking passengers (riding behind the driver) from one village to another for a fee.

Houses along the way are mainly made of *palma*, a board cut from a palm trunk. Their roofs are of thatch or zinc (tin). They are often painted turquoise or pink, with contrasting window frames and doors. Pink (or rose) and turquoise is the most common color combination, but there are also yellow, green, and blue in various combinations. Some houses are not painted. The better houses are of concrete block, also painted in the same colorful combinations.

The nearer one gets to Azua, the shorter is the vegetation, consisting mostly of "scrub" brush and more and more cactus. Stands by the roadside are sparser, and they have less fruit. Mostly they sell broom heads, made from a type of palm frond. Broomsticks are sold separately, made from long, slender limbs that have been stripped and smoothed. No longer are there many cattle--goats are more common. There are also motor scooters and burros, and trucks filled with tomatoes, charcoal, or plantains on the way to Santo Domingo. Automobile traffic is light.

The economic base of the Azua region is agricultural, and in recent years it has been stimulated by the development of the Canal Yaque del Sur-Azua, which brings water to the area, making possible the irrigation of crops. In response to the increased water availability, a number of large companies moved to the area in the 1970s, initiating large-scale food-crop operations, partly for export and partly for the domestic market. The main crops of these companies are melons and tomatoes. In addition, there are many very small farming operations that grow plantains, bananas, corn, beans, and other crops for local or domestic consumption. In the higher areas of the cordillera, there is also some coffee production.

The population of the province of Azua grew from 90,590 inhabitants in 1970 to 142,770 in 1981, an increase of 57.6 percent. This represents the third highest growth percentage for that period of all 27 provinces, with only the Distrito Nacional (Santo Domingo) and La Romana showing higher rates. No doubt the Azua growth was due to the irrigation projects and subsequent agribusiness developments. The population of the country as a whole increased by 41 percent over that period (Censo Nacional, 1981). Most of the inhabitants of the Azua region are said to be descendants of the Canary Island slaves brought to the island in the sixteenth century, with the opening of sugar plantations (*Enciclopedia dominicana* 1978).

The Azua Valley is generally less well off, in terms of its economic and human resources, than other regions of the country. For example, data from the National Census of 1981 show that the literacy rate for the subregion (the Southwestern Valley) was 52.5 percent (for the population aged five years or older), much lower than the 69.4 percent literacy rate for the country as a whole. Statistics on school experience mirror this difference. For the Southwestern Valley, the percentage of those over age five who had never attended school was 65 percent, compared with 47 percent for the country as a whole. On these measures, there was little difference in the rates for males and females. Thus, the region of the study has a relatively low educational level, even for a country that has lower educational and literacy levels than most other Latin American and Caribbean countries (Curtin 1982).

The Manpower Survey of 1980 (ONE 1980) shows that the Southwest also had the highest unemployment rates among rural women of all regions of the country (63.4 percent, compared with 57.7 percent for the Southeast and 47.5 percent for the Cibao). Other data in that report show that many rural women of every region would like to work, but they do not believe that there are jobs available to them. As mentioned in Chapter 1, the rate of rural male unemployment (9.3 percent) in the Southwest was the lowest of the three regions, while the rate for rural women was the highest. The Manpower Survey also shows that the unemployment rate for rural women (for the country as a whole) is highest in the teen years and early twenties, falling steadily for older cohorts. We can probably safely assume that this pattern holds for the Azua Valley as well. Thus, due to the harsh environment, the lack of natural resources, and the high levels of unemployment, this region has been one of poverty and bare subsistence.

A survey of a group of farmers in the Azua area showed that they considered the lack of economic resources (especially the lack of credit) and the scarcity of water to be the two most severe of the many problems facing them. They needed to borrow money to plant and harvest crops, but the conditions of credit offered to them were very unfavorable, reducing their ability to earn a living. The shortage of water is a problem, even though there are now irrigation canals in their area. Due in part to lack of organization of the use of water, many farmers regularly lose their crops for lack of water (DeLaine 1987).

In the last few years, several large private agricultural production companies have set up operations in the Azua area. These companies are primarily dedicated to the production of melons for export and/or tomatoes for use in tomato paste, mainly for the domestic market. Among the most important of these are ABC and DoMex (export-oriented companies) and Barcelo (which grows tomatoes for the domestic market). The headquarters of DoMex is located near some of the communities studied. These companies all recruit workers from most of the communities in the general area, some providing transportation in trucks for fieldworkers.

These companies vary in their work organization and policies. The tomato-producing companies tend to hire more fieldworkers, while the melon companies often contract with individual farmers to do much of the fieldwork. However, all of the companies do hire local labor, often providing jobs to people who probably would not have work otherwise. Among the workers hired by the companies are a number of women. The melon-producing companies usually hire women as "processors" of produce--packers, for example. Other women are hired as janitors or cooks for the rest of the workers. The tomato companies use more women as fieldworkers--planters or pickers--as well as processors. Most of this work is seasonal, taking place in the early months of the year. However, it does provide employment opportunities for women that were not available before.

The present study attempts to assess some of the basic characteristics of the women of the rural Azua area, both the typical women of the communities studied and those who have begun working for the large companies. In the following chapters, we will be discussing various aspects of the lives of a representative sample of the women of the small communities in the area, as well as corresponding aspects of the lives of a sample of women who work for the agricultural companies. It is hoped that the information herein will provide some basic knowledge of the women of the region, as well as insights into the effects of paid employment for rural women on their levels of living, families, and hopes and aspirations for the future.

3   Procedures:
Carrying out the Survey

The survey study of women in rural communities in the Azua region, which forms the basis of this book, was carried out in the summer of 1986 and spring of 1987. In this chapter the principal procedures used in carrying out the research are discussed.

SELECTION AND TRAINING OF INTERVIEWERS

Once the questionnaire was developed and initial trips to the communities had been made, we needed to select and train interviewers to do the survey. For this part of the study, I had a research associate, a native Dominican who had studied in the United States and was familiar both with local customs and with training of personnel. We wanted to find a group of women from communities similar to those to be studied, who were able to read the questionnaire well and understand the general instructions and the purposes of the study. A group of 17 initial trainees was identified for us by a local sociologist who had been working in the area on a government water-use evaluation project. All of these young women were from the local communities near Azua, and all had completed at least three years of high school. (This put them well above average for their communities.) We met with each group of three to five women in their respective communities and invited them to come to a training session on the following day. A classroom had been arranged at the local library in Azua as the place for the training. All 17 of those we initially met came to the training session.

As so often happens in settings such as this, things did not go exactly as planned. The library head had told us we could have the classroom from 1:30 to 6:00, but when we arrived, we found the library closed. We waited until 2:00, when some of the women thought the library would open. We spoke to others who thought it would open at 2:30 or 3:00. (The latter was correct.) Fortunately, we knew of a conference room in the offices of the water-use project where our sociologist contact was, so we quickly went there to ask permission to use that space. They were able to let us use it, so we and our 17 trainees walked the three blocks to that office and were able to begin within 45 minutes of our planned starting time. Events such as this were common in our experience, and we tried to maintain an attitude of flexibility and a sense of humor about it all.

We began the training session by giving each woman a pencil, a copy of our instructions about interviewing (see Appendix A), and a small notebook that she would use for taking notes about each interview completed. We introduced ourselves, explained the purpose of the study, and then went over the main points of interview technique: how they should introduce themselves to their subjects, how to identify the right person to interview, the importance of maintaining an attitude of neutrality, and so forth. All of the points on the interviewing instructions were covered and explained. During the discussion, questions were encouraged and at various points the trainees were asked to explain to the group what we had just covered. At other times, they were asked to "role-play" to demonstrate, for example, how to introduce oneself and explain the purpose of the study to the potential respondent. Overall, the women were attentive, asked good questions, and appeared to be interested and competent.

After going over the interview instructions, we then went over the questionnaire itself, question by question, explaining how to mark answers, what to do in various contingencies, and so on. We asked that each of them practice that night by interviewing someone at home (a sister, a neighbor, or their compatriot interviewer in their community).

Then we gave them each two more interview schedules and asked them to do two additional interviews within the next three days with women in communities we designated. These interviews represented our own "pretest" of our questionnaire, and also gave our trainees practice in the field before doing the actual study. The communities designated for these interviews were near the home communities of the interviewers but were not to be sampled for the actual study.

We gave each interviewer-trainee RD$5 as an advance to cover any transportation costs they might incur. They were to receive a total of RD$35 for participating in the training period (when they returned with the two completed questionnaires).

We met with the trainees as planned at 10 a.m. on Tuesday, July 8. All were present, and this time the library was open. We first asked for comments about their experiences in the pretest. After discussing their problems and questions with them, we dismissed them for an hour so we could go over each interviewer's work so as to identify further problems. We found 5 of the 17 to have done relatively poor work, misinterpreting questions, skipping portions of the questionnaire, writing illegibly, and so forth. They were not given further assignments. Two or three of the remaining 12 were weak, but we thought they could be trained, so we kept them but spent extra time explaining their errors. We also watched them more closely during the data-gathering phase. The remaining nine did good work with relatively few errors, and we felt that they could do well with minimal extra training. We arranged to meet each group in its own community on the following Friday.

PRETEST REVISIONS AND INITIAL INTERVIEWS

During the next two days, we revised the questionnaire[1] slightly, according to the results of the field test of the two "practice" interviews. We then had 150 copies prepared. In addition, we analyzed in more detail the problems that the 12 interviewers had, and we prepared a second list of instructions that covered the most common or serious types of errors made. We made copies of these for all interviewers, even though not everyone had made all of the errors. These were given to each interviewer on Friday, along with ten questionnaires and instructions on how to select households. In addition, we explained the problems verbally to the women, paying special attention to those who had been weakest in the field test.

---

[1] A copy of the final questionnaire is translated in Appendix B, and in the original Spanish in Appendix C.

We made a date to return five days later to collect the first completed questionnaires and to answer any further questions, as well as to check on their procedures and to catch any further errors that might arise.

THE SAMPLING PROCEDURE

The communities that we chose are small and agricultural, containing from 51 to 599 households. Ansonia, La Ceiba, Las Barias, and Los Jobillos lie along the road that goes south from Highway 2 west of Azua and connects to the road going past the DoMex operation. Along that road are Guayacanal and Pueblo Viejo. These two villages, being closer to DoMex, have more people working for that company. The houses are not neatly laid out along well-designed streets, but are scattered in a seemingly random manner. There usually is a main road that runs through the town (or along its edge), and other dirt paths/roads that allow access to other parts of the community.

The communities appear to be homogeneous in terms of social level of living--there are no "better" or "worse" areas; all streets look similar in this respect. There are a few better houses on any street, and many poor ones. Almost all have walls of *palma*--boards made from the split trunks of palm trees--and thatch roofs. The difference in level of living can be measured in part by whether the house has a floor of concrete or of dirt.

Given the homogeneity of the communities' households, plus the difficulty of devising a sampling scheme in the absence of housenumbers, streets, and orderly placement of housing, we decided that a systematic sample would be easiest to accomplish and would approximate a random sample.

Each interviewer was assigned a section of the community (one side of the main road, for example) to sample. She was told to take every nth household, beginning at the edge of her area and counting all houses--including those behind and down "paths." The n was selected so as to have the correct sample size from each community, and was figured by dividing the desired sample size into the number of households located in each community. This information was available from a 1985 survey of the Regional Health Department for these communities. For example, we wanted 30 interviews from Pueblo Viejo, and there are 599 households there, so we instructed the interviewers to select every nineteenth household ($599/30 = 19.9$).

Just as the communities internally were homogeneous, so there appeared to be little difference between most of the communities. Los Jobillos, nearer to Azua, was somewhat more "urban" than the rest, having more than one small food store (*colmado*), a dining place (*comedor*), and numbered houses. However, it was inhabited predominantly by agricultural people. All the communities are near each other, but only two are close enough to the main large companies to have many people employed there (Pueblo Viejo and Guayacanal).

Interviews were carried out with the principal woman of each household selected, either the female head or the wife of a male head. After completing the original 120 interviews, we found that only two members of the sample of women had worked for the companies. We then instructed the best interviewers to return to the same villages and find a purposive sample of 30 more women who had worked as laborers for the agricultural companies during the past year. With these, we can better assess the effects of this type of work on family welfare and roles. In addition, we can compare these women with those in the systematic samples to see how they differ from the typical women.

This sample was selected by asking those women already interviewed who worked for one of the companies for names of others with whom they worked, and in turn asking those to point out others. Although this type of sampling sometimes leads to a biased sample (because only the acquaintances of a few lead people are selected), we did not believe this to be a problem here, since we had several initial leads. We also had the capability of comparing these women with the original sample of the villages, to see if they were unrepresentative in background characteristics.

OTHER METHODOLOGICAL PROCEDURES

The initial phase of interviewing the community sample took place in July 1986. The interviewing of women workers was done in two stages; the first was in July and August 1986. In that stage, 29 usable interviews were completed. The second stage of worker interviews was in March 1987, during the working season. In that period, 61 more workers were interviewed. All of the analyses presented here are for the 69 workers who were the "primary women" of their household, since that was the person interviewed in the community sample.

The interviewers were very effective, completing all except one of the first 150 interviews attempted, giving us a refusal rate of only 0.7 percent. Only one of the interviewers had some serious problems, so that three of her ten completed interviews had to be discarded. In August, a coding schema was developed and the coding of data began. Due to the complex nature of the data and the relatively large number of "open" questions whose responses had to be carefully read and "content analyzed" before coding, I carried out this process myself. It was a long and tedious process, taking some two and a half months to complete.

The survey data were then analyzed, partly by statistical techniques and partly through content analysis of open-ended questions. Due to the richness of the information, quantitative comparisons are simple, largely descriptive in purpose. For all analyses, percentage distributions are compared between the two samples, the "community" and the "worker." The data for the community sample act as a control or comparison group, which will help to interpret the results from the worker sample. If only workers had been studied, we would not know if they had certain traits because they were workers, or because everyone in that community had those traits. Hence, for the purposes of seeing exactly what types of women become employed by these companies, and what characteristics are associated with paid employment, it is necessary to have the comparison group that is not employed. Differences between the two groups might be attributed to the employment differences, since on other characteristics they are similar.

In addition to the survey results, much of the following analysis is based on observations made in the communities, which I visited on a number of occasions. The interviewers were very useful as informants as well. Overall, I believe that the combination of qualitative and quantitative techniques has made this study not only more valid but more interesting as well.

Background Characteristics
of Respondents

This chapter has two purposes. The first is to describe the women of the area sampled, using data from the original community sample. This sample was chosen so as to be representative of the populations of communities studied or, more precisely, the principal women of community households. Thus, results from that sample should give us information about the women of the communities studied-- who they are, where they came from, their household situation, and other characteristics.

The second purpose is to compare the women in the community sample with the sample of women workers employed by the large agricultural companies in the area. By doing this comparison, we shall be able to see what types of women are working for the companies--are they representative of their communities, or do they differ in significant ways in their backgrounds? We will present data for both groups on age, education completed, husband's education, migration history, place of birth, age at marriage, household size, and religious participation in this chapter.

AGE DISTRIBUTION

The distribution of ages of the women in the two samples is given in Table 4.1. The community sample includes more women in the older (above 40) age groups, while the workers are more concentrated in the younger ages,

Table 4.1
Age Distribution of Women in the Two Samples

Age	Community sample		Worker sample	
	n	%	n	%
Under 20	0	0.0	2	2.9
20-24	9	7.7	6	8.6
25-29	19	16.2	25	35.7
30-34	17	14.5	15	21.4
35-39	21	17.9	9	12.9
40-44	13	11.1	4	5.7
45-49	11	9.4	5	7.1
50-54	20	17.1	2	2.9
55-59	2	1.7	2	2.9
60 and over	5	4.3	0	0.0
Totals	117	99.9	70	100.1
Median age:		37		30.2
Mean age:		39.2		32.4

especially in the ages 25-35. That age range contains only 30.7 percent of the women in the representative sample, but 57.1 percent of the worker sample. Both groups had similar age ranges, but the means and medians were about 7 years lower for the worker group, due to the greater concentration in the 25-35 range. The workers are more likely to be young adults, but they come from diverse age groups ranging from 18 to 59. The data suggest that women over 40 are not employed as frequently as younger women in this type of work, even though they do represent about one-fifth of the workers studied. The reason that more younger women were not found in the samples is that these women are the "principal women" of their respective households, and age is one factor that increases the likelihood of being in that position. However, since almost all women become "principal women" of separate households at marriage, and since almost all women marry by age 25, this sample is fairly close to being representative of all adult women in the communities.

EDUCATION

The educational attainment of women in the Dominican Republic has already been described as very low, and the region of the Azua Valley as lower than average. In the community sample (Table 4.2), we can see that 30 percent of these women did not attend school at all (or completed first grade). Of those attending school, the greatest number (38 percent of the sample) completed three or four years. Only 8 percent went beyond sixth grade, and only one woman completed high school. Thus, on the average, these women have relatively little formal education, showing a median of three years.

The worker sample is only a little better off. Only 13.2 percent had no formal education, compared with 28.7 percent of the community sample. However, these women were only slightly more likely to have gone beyond primary level, and only one had attended high school. Their median educational level was four years (instead of three). Overall the two groups are very similar in their educational levels, if they went to school at all.

The main advantage that the workers had in terms of their greater percentage having attended school was in their ability to read and write. (Incidentally, no difference was found in these measures--everyone who said she could read also said she could write, and vice versa). The figures at the bottom of Table 4.2 show that while only 68 percent of the community sample could read, almost 85 percent of the worker sample was able to do so. These percentages correspond roughly to the percentages who completed at least one year of school. Even one year seems to have led to a level of reading sufficient for these women to claim literacy. It seems probable that the main source of this difference comes from the larger percentage of older women in the community sample, as they would be most likely never to have attended school at all.

Table 4.2
Educational Attainment and Literacy of Women
in the Two Samples (last grade completed)

Last grade completed	Community sample		Worker sample	
	n	%	n	%
None	33	28.7	9	13.2
First	2	1.7	1	1.5
Second	10	8.7	10	14.7
Third	22	19.1	15	22.1
Fourth	22	19.1	13	19.1
Fifth	12	10.4	9	13.2
Sixth	5	4.3	2	2.9
Seventh/Eighth	5	4.3	8	11.8
Ninth/Eleventh	3	2.6	1	1.5
Twelfth	1	0.9	0	0.0
Totals	115	99.8	68	100.0
Percent able to read:		68.1		84.6

HUSBAND'S EDUCATION

For those respondents who currently were married, the
level of their husbands' education was asked. The responses
to this are presented in Table 4.3. In the community sample,
27.7 percent of the husbands had had no formal education,
very similar to the 28.7 percent figure for the women.
Although most had completed only three or four years of
primary school, a few (15.9 percent) had gone beyond
primary level, and 6.4 percent had completed high school.
Thus the husbands were slightly more likely than their wives
to have gone to intermediate or secondary school (the figure

Table 4.3
Husbands' Last Grade Completed, by Sample,
Married or In-Union Respondents Only (percentages)

Years completed	Community sample	Worker sample
None	27.7	8.9
1 - 2	7.4	2.2
3 - 4	35.1	48.9
5 - 6	13.8	13.3
7 - 8	7.4	13.3
9 - 11	2.1	4.4
12 or more	6.4	8.9
Totals	99.9	99.9
(n)	(94)	(45)

Percent able to read:

| | 72.6 | 88.9 |

for wives was 7.8 percent), although on the whole, the distributions are similar.

The husbands of the worker group were, like their spouses, somewhat better educated. A smaller percentage had no education (8.9 percent), and a larger percentage (26.6 percent) had studied beyond the primary level. Similarly, the percent able to read is higher for the workers' husbands, approximately equal to the percent completing one school year. For both groups of husbands, the modal category was three-four years, and such differences as exist are slight.

BIRTHPLACE, MIGRATION

The women were asked where they were born, and their responses were classified as "local area" or "away from local area." These categories were loosely defined, but the "local area" in general means any place within the *municipio* of Azua.

To be classified as "outside the local area," the birthplace had to be in, for example, the area of Barahona or Elias Piña. Even though some of the women were born outside the local area, they were usually from adjacent provinces within 40 or 50 miles of their present community. About 85 percent of the women in this study were born in the local area--usually in the same or a neighboring community. There were no differences in the two samples on this, meaning that the women who work for the large companies are not migrants to the area from other regions. Even though the population of the region has been growing rapidly, most of the in-migrants are apparently not moving into these rural communities.

The responses to the question "Where have you lived?" were classified in two ways: first, according to the number of different places lived; and second, according to whether any of those places were outside the local area. The responses show that most women in the community sample had been relatively stable, with 43.6 percent having lived their entire lives in their present communities and another 34 percent having lived in only one other place. Only 22 percent had lived in three or more communities.

By comparison, the working women were somewhat more mobile; 35 percent had lived in three or more places, although for most of these it was three and not more. Still, the women in the worker sample are perhaps drawn more from those who are less tied to the community because of having lived elsewhere. A higher percentage of these women had lived outside of the local area, some in Santo Domingo or other cities.

With respect to the length of time the woman had lived in the local community, the community women were very stable, with over three-fourths having lived in their community for 20 years or more. Only 8 percent of these women had lived there for less than ten years. This suggests that the traditional and usual pattern is for the women in these communities to live their entire lives within the same community, perhaps moving once (probably at marriage).

By contrast, the women in the worker sample are more likely to have been in the community for shorter periods, with 21 percent having lived there for less than 10 years, and about half less than 20 years. Some of this difference is a function of age differences in the two samples, but much of it is probably due to the greater mobility of the worker sample. This greater mobility may have led these women to see employment as an option for them, since they might have seen women working for wages in other places (especially if they lived in cities). They also might have been in those other places as domestic servants, getting used to the idea of earning money. Finally, they would perhaps be less controlled by community norms, having spent less time there and having experienced different norms in other locations.

AGE AT FIRST MARITAL UNION

The women were asked at what age they left their parents' home, and for what purpose. They were also asked at what age they first married or formed a union with a man. For almost everyone there was no difference in the age at leaving the parents' home and the age of marriage. They left home for the purpose of marriage or union. Only 7 women out of the 187 in the survey left home to work, and another left to live with her grandparents. Therefore, for practical purposes the age at which these women moved out of their parents' homes was the age at first union. It is interesting to note that they all *did* leave their parents' home at marriage or union. In no case did a husband move into his wife's family's home, and none of the respondents' households included sons-in-law (although there were a few daughters-in-law living with an adult son in the household). The residence pattern, then, shows strong preference for new couples to have their own households, with a tendency toward patrilocality (the wife moves to the husband's family's house) as an accepted option when independence is not possible.

The responses to the question about age at first marital union are presented in Table 4.4. The data show that the marriage ages of these women were very young, by most standards. The earliest age given was 11 years, and four more members of the community sample had married at 12. After that, the numbers marrying at each age tend to increase until age 17, the most common marriage age. By the end of the seventeenth year, 62.7 percent of these women had married. By the end of the twentieth year, 92.3 percent had married, and all had married by age 26.

In comparing the worker sample with the community sample, the only difference is a tendency for the workers to have married at slightly later ages, if they married in their teens. For example, comparing the cumulative distributions, one can see that while 21 percent of the community sample had married before age 15, only 11.5 percent of the worker women had. These figures rapidly converge, however, as

Table 4.4
Age at First Marital Union, by Sample
(percentages and cumulative percentages)

	Community sample		Worker sample	
Age	%	Cum.%	%	Cum.%
11	0.9	0.9	0.0	0.0
12	3.5	4.4	1.4	1.4
13	7.0	11.4	2.9	4.3
14	9.6	21.0	7.2	11.5
15	7.8	28.8	18.8	30.3
16	13.9	42.7	13.0	43.3
17	20.0	62.7	10.1	53.4
18	11.3	74.0	18.8	72.2
19	9.6	83.6	11.6	83.8
20	8.7	92.3	10.1	93.9
21	1.7	94.0	4.3	98.2
22	2.6	96.6	1.4	99.6
23	0.0	96.6	----	----
24	1.7	98.3	----	----
25	1.7	100.0	----	----
Totals	100.0		99.6	
(n)	(115)		(69)	

almost 75 percent of each group had married by the end of the eighteenth year, and almost all by age 21. On this characteristic, then, the two samples are very similar. The greater percentage of very young marriages in the community sample may be another effect of the difference in age, if women of older cohorts tended to marry at younger ages. For both groups, however, the median age at first marriage was 17 years.

HOUSEHOLD SIZE

The household size (number of people living in the household) of the women in the community sample ranged from 2 to 15, with a mean of 6.9 and a median and mode of 7. Thus, these households typically had a large number of people to support. By comparison, the worker households were smaller, though not a great deal smaller. The range for their household sizes was from 2 to 18, but the mean of 5.7 and the median of 5 were smaller than the corresponding figures for the community sample. The workers' households had the largest proportion in the range two-four, with most others spread over the five-ten range. The most common size for the community sample's households was in the six-eight range. Again, this is partly, but not completely, an effect of age differences, with younger women having fewer children at home. It is also an effect of different family patterns--as we shall see later, the worker group contains a larger percentage of mother-child families, which tend to have fewer children as well as one less adult in the household.

RELIGIOUS PARTICIPATION

As a final set of background comparisons, the two groups of women are compared according to religious participation. It is often believed that religion plays an important role in women's decisions about family and fertility matters, for example, so this information will be useful in interpreting other results.

Respondents were asked how often they attend church, either for mass or for other purposes. Although the great majority said they had been baptized Catholic (over 90 percent), only 11 percent of the community sample and 18 percent of the workers said they attend mass at least weekly. About 26-30 percent attend at least once a month, but the majority of both groups (about 65 percent) said they attend only once a year or less. Fully half said they "never or rarely" attend church. Of those "rarely" attending, the purpose of attending was sometimes given as "to baptize the children."

The husbands were even less likely to participate in religious services, with only 5 percent of the community sample husbands attending once a month or more frequently. Over 80 percent of the husbands were said to attend church never or only rarely.

The lack of official participation in church activities does not mean that the women were not "religious." The majority (59 percent) claimed that they pray at least a few times a week, with 34 percent praying every day. Thus, for the women in these communities religion is a personal faith but not a social activity. Official church teachings probably have little impact on their lives.

SUMMARY

The data presented in this chapter have described the ages, educational attainments, birthplaces and migration patterns, ages at first marriage, husbands' education, household size, and religious practice of the sample of the six communities in the Azua region. In addition, comparisons have been made on these same characteristics with women in the worker sample. The workers differed from the women in the community sample in the following ways: they (the workers) were less likely to be over 35 in age and more likely to be in the 25-35 age group. They were more likely to have had some formal education, but not significantly more likely to have gone beyond the primary level. Similarly, they were more likely to be literate. They showed some evidence of having moved around more in their lives and to have lived for a shorter time in their communities. They were somewhat less likely to have married at an extremely young age (before 15). If they were married, their husbands were more likely to have gone to school and to have gone beyond the primary level. And their households were, on the average, smaller. On place of birth, the two groups were virtually identical, as they were on religious practice.

On most of these measures, there were strong similarities between the two samples, and the differences that did show up were not great. Many of the background differences found probably reflect the age difference in the groups. They do not suggest that the worker group was greatly different from other members of the community, except in being more heavily concentrated in the ages 25-35, and in having been somewhat more likely to have lived in more than one place within the local area.

5   Land, Agriculture, and Employment: Resources for Survival

The majority of the people in this study are involved in agriculture, the traditional source of subsistence for people in these communities. In this chapter, we will describe the agricultural resources and activities of the families represented by the samples. Then we will turn to a discussion of other kinds of employment: wage labor or income-generating nonagricultural activities. We will describe the two samples on a number of characteristics having to do with the generation of income. As in the previous chapter, the data from the community sample are assumed to represent the community as a whole, while the worker sample represents only those women who work as laborers for the large agribusiness firms in the area.

LAND TENURE

The basis of farming is land. One must have access to land if one is to earn a living, or to subsist in a self-sufficient way, on a farm. The women in the study were asked how much land their families owned, as well as how much they actually cultivated. Table 5.1 gives the results of the landownership question. In the community sample, just over a third of the families had no land. The median landholding category for the 74 families who owned some land was 20-29 *tareas* (3.2-4.7 acres). Only 12 percent of all families in this sample owned as many as 50 *tareas* (8 acres).

Table 5.1
Landownership of Families in Samples

N. tareas	Community sample	Worker sample
None	36.8	69.6
1 - 9	8.5	2.9
10 - 19	21.4	10.1
20 - 29	9.4	5.8
30 - 39	7.7	4.3
40 - 49	4.3	4.3
50 and more	12.0	2.9
	100.1	99.9
(n)	(117)	(69)

When we compare the landholdings of the worker group with those of the representative sample, we see a great difference. About 69 percent of the workers' families had no land, compared with 37 percent of the community sample families. The women who work for the larger companies come predominantly from families with no land resources, so that wage labor is more of a necessity. Of those workers from families owning land, the distribution of landholdings was similar to that of the community sample, the main difference being in the greater percentage with no land.

The community sample members were also asked how many *tareas* of land the family actually cultivated. This number was often less than the number owned. Some 51 families cultivated no land, even though 8 of these families owned some land. And, as another example, although 14 families owned over 50 *tareas*, only 9 families cultivated that much. In addition, some families cultivated land but did not own any, working on other people's land.

Of the 68 families who cultivated crops, two-thirds had legal title to their land, while another 25 percent "owned" their land but had no title to it. A few families had other tenancy arrangements; 7.4 percent worked land that was either rented, loaned, or sharecropped. In this region, then, sharing or tenant farming is not common. Those who own no land tend to work as laborers or employees, but not as decision-making farmers.

For the active farming group, the principal crops grown were tomatoes, plantains, corn, and bananas. Most of them cultivated crops for sale to others as an income-generating activity. Only 10 percent of the active cultivators said that their crops were for their own consumption only. The rest grew crops for sale only (31.3 percent) or for both consumption and sale (58.2 percent).

Cattle were kept by 44 of the families in the community sample (37.6 percent of the families), although most of them had only one or two cows (probably milk cows). Only 8 percent (10 families) had more than 5 cattle, the largest herd being 25.

The respondents were asked if their family's main source of income was the farm or "other activities." The farm was said to be the principal source of income for less than half (46.4 percent) of the families in the community sample. Even many of those who owned some land and farmed it, then, had to rely on other activities as their primary income source.

Of the women in the worker sample, only 22 percent reported farming to be their family's primary source of income. Their lack of land to farm explains in part their movement into the labor force.

EMPLOYMENT OUTSIDE THE FARM

One of the main purposes of this study is to look at the impacts on families of women's outside employment for wages. The data in the community sample will give us an idea of the incidence within the community of this type of activity and of other wage-earning activities of the families in these communities.

Those data show that the percentage of women working for pay outside the home is very low. Only 14 of the 117 (12 percent) were employed at some time during the previous year. Of those, only two worked for large agricultural companies, the others being in such traditional occupations as self-employed makers/sellers of fried foods or sweets (four), street vendors (two), domestic/janitorial work (two), or small business owners (*colmado* owners). One was a teacher (see Table 5.2). Thus, the overall incidence of women working for

Table 5.2
Occupations of Community Sample Respondents
and Their Husbands

Respondents (n=117)			Husbands (n=96)		
Nonemployed	103	(88.0%)	Nonemployed	60	(62.5%)
Employed	14	(12.0%)	Employed	36	(37.5%)
Food vendor	4		Day laborer	8	(22.2%)
Domestic,			Produce processor	4	(11.1%)
cleaning	2		Guard	4	(11.1%)
Street vendor	2		Driver	3	(8.3%)
Produce			Tractor, machine		
processor	2		operator	2	(5.6%)
Small			Pump operator	2	(5.6%)
business	2		Teacher	2	(5.6%)
Lottery sales	1		Supervisor of		
Teacher	1		food processor	1	(2.8%)
			Colmado	1	(2.8%)
			Head mechanic	1	(2.8%)
			Tobacco buyer	1	(2.8%)
			Mechanic	1	(2.8%)
			Natl. Guard	1	(2.8%)
			Foreman-planting	1	(2.8%)
			Radio repairs	1	(2.8%)
			Other	3	(8.3%)

agribusiness companies is very low, less than 3 percent of the community sample. Though all of the women in the community samples working for agricultural companies were from the two nearest villages, Pueblo Viejo and Guayacanal, they represented only 5 percent of the samples from those communities. Thus, in terms of provision of employment for a large proportion of women, the companies have not had much impact.

As might be expected, a larger percentage of husbands was employed outside the farm. Of 96 husbands (*maridos*) in the sample, 36 (37.5 percent) had worked for income during the past year. Of these, 13 worked for the agricultural companies. The largest group of these men (7) came from Guayacanal, the only village in which the majority of employed men were employed by the companies. These seven represent 21 percent of the families sampled in that village. The men working for the companies held various types of jobs, including a few supervisory positions or work with machinery, for example (Table 5.2). Thus, the impact on women of the companies' activities in these communities is perhaps felt more through its employment of their husbands, brothers, or fathers than through their own employment. This pattern could increase or maintain the dependency of women on the male members of their families. It may or may not improve the women's standard of living, depending on such factors as the extent to which the husbands share their resources with the women and families.

The most common occupation of the other male workers was that of day laborer (held by eight men), followed by a variety of mostly unskilled or semiskilled jobs (night watchman, driver, fireman). There were two teachers in this group. In addition, there were 12 cases in which another member of the family worked outside the farm for income. In 11 cases, these workers were male (sons), and in one case a family had both a male and a female income earner other than the respondent or her husband. In 3 of these 12 cases, the "other" family member worked for an agricultural company.

Multiple income earners within households were rare, but could be found. In five cases, both partners (husband and wife) worked for pay, and there were two others in which the husband and another member of the household worked. In the great majority of cases, however, only one person per household was employed, and that person was usually the husband of the respondent. In all, 55 of the 117 households sampled (47 percent) had at least one income earner for at least part of the year previous to the interview. At the same time, half of the households had no employed members.

Salaries (or the earnings of those who were self-employed) were stated by 13 of the women workers in the community sample. These were monthly earnings during the months in which they were working. They ranged from RD$30 to RD$500, with a median of RD$230 per month. At an exchange rate of 2.75, the rate at the time of the interview, this comes out to be about US$84 per month. Since almost all of these women, other than the two company workers, are self-employed, these are crude estimates of average earnings.

However, the work of the women is often seasonal--they do not work during all months. Of 13 who gave this information, 8 said they worked 12 months a year, the other 5 working from 6 to 10 months. Of the 14 workers, 10 said that they were still working at the time of the interview (July 1986).

Salaries of husbands who were employed tended to be a little higher, though not much. The range was from RD$50 per month to over RD$1,000, although only 2 of the 36 earned more than RD$400. The most common salary, as well as the median salary, was RD$250, earned by 16 of the 36 employed husbands, or about US$90 per month.

Men's work is more likely to be year-round, as 76 percent of the working husbands were reported to have worked 12 months of the year (26 of 34 responses). The others had mostly worked from 6 to 10 months, with only one working less than 6 months. Almost all (94 percent) of the husbands who had been employed at all during the year were still working at the time of the interview. Thus, a significant proportion of households, though less than half, potentially has fairly steady income from the employment of husbands, wives, sons, or daughters.

The women in the special worker sample, of course, all had earnings during the past year. The majority of these women worked as packers or sorters of melons or tomatoes, with a few others in other positions (Table 5.3). One had a supervisory position. Their salaries ranged from RD$140 to RD$522 monthly, with RD$280 (US$102) being the median. The middle 50 percent of women were earning between RD$220 and RD$300 per month, with 25 percent earning more than RD$300 and 25 percent earning less than RD$220.

Most of these women toiled long hours during the working months, reporting from 12 to 84 hours per week, the median being 56 hours per week (reported by 11 respondents). The seasonal nature of their work can be seen in the fact that the majority of respondents worked only 3 or 4 months during the year. (Out of 65 giving this information, 27 worked 3 or 4 months, 1 worked 5 months, and 24 worked 6 months. Only 4 respondents reported working for 12 months.) Hence, though salaries are relatively good when compared with those of women or their husbands of the other sample, the yearly earnings are usually much less and are concentrated in a short period of three to six months of the year. Only five women said they were still working at the time of the July interview.

The women of the worker sample are more likely to have husbands who are employed than are the women of the community sample. Twenty-seven respondents, making up 38.6 percent of the sample (56.2 percent of the married respondents), had husbands who worked for wages or earned income from self-employment. The women come from families that are less likely to be involved in family farming than the average family in the community. The occupations of these husbands are listed in Table 5.3. Eighteen (67

Table 5.3
Occupations of Worker Sample Respondents and
Their Husbands

Respondents (n=70)			Husbands (n=48)		
Nonemployed	0		Nonemployed	21	(43.8%)
Employed	70		Employed	27	(56.2%)
Produce processor	44	(62.8%)	Produce processor	7	
Weeding, fieldwork	11	(15.9%)	Supervisor	3	
Picking tomatoes/melons	5	(7.1%)	Day laborer	2	
Janitor	2	(2.9%)	Guard	2	
Supervisor of packing	1	(1.4%)	Driver	2	
Cook	1	(1.4%)	Vendor	1	
Machine operator	1	(1.4%)	Small business	1	
Other	5	(7.1%)	Plumber	1	
			Supervisor of fuels	1	
Total	70		Rum promoter	1	
			National Guard	1	
			Mechanic	1	
			"Concho" driver	1	
			Pump operator	1	
			Carpenter	1	
			Melon picker	1	
			Total	27	

percent of the 27 employed husbands) were employed by the large agricultural companies, most of the others being self-employed. Hence, the majority of the married women who are employed by the companies are married to men who work for wages. In a few cases, these families tend to have more than one source of income (if the workers are married).

The husbands' salaries (only 10 were reported) range from RD$150 to RD$350, with RD$300 (US$109) being the median and the mode. Unlike their wives, however, most of the men were employed for 12 months of the year (8 of the 10 reporting this information). In these families, then, the husband's earnings still greatly outweigh those of wife.

In ten families, other members of the household also were working, six for the large companies. In over half of these cases, the other family member was female, usually a single daughter who lived at home. Thus, those who work for the companies often seem to be able to have more than one family member involved--perhaps because the original workers find out about openings, or because they decide to apply together, or because these families have rejected as a whole the notion that women should not work outside the home.

OTHER SOURCES OF INCOME

We have seen that a little less than half of the women in the community sample said that the farm was the family's main source of income, and that about 45 percent of families had at least one income earner outside the farm. Other sources of income are help given by relatives and pensions, social security, and so forth. This type of income is usually small and not always steady, but it may be critical to the very-low-income families who receive it. Respondents were asked if they received help from these sources.

Some 21 percent of community sample families were receiving aid from relatives. Almost half of these were receiving help from relatives living in another country, many in the United States. This pattern of intrafamily help is very important in the Dominican Republic, as sons and daughters who move away to find work send part of their earnings home to the parental family.

Only two families received any kind of government aid or pensions. Thus the primary "welfare institution" for these families is the extended family.

In the worker sample, only five families were receiving any aid, all from relatives in another country. Thus, they were much less likely than the community sample members to receive this sort of aid. We can guess that as people grow older, they are more likely to receive this sort of aid, as children leave home and send money back.

In another question concerning the migration of members of the household, this helping relationship was confirmed. Of 30 families in the community sample who reported having had a family member leave the household to live elsewhere, 17 said that member helped, either by directly sending money or by buying things for them.

SUMMARY

In summary, then, the people of the rural communities near Azua tend to depend primarily on the work of men for their cash income--either in their farm work or in employment. Only a small proportion of women are employed, although it is probable that more would take jobs if they were available. The sample of workers differed in this respect, in that many came from two-earner families. Although their work was less steady than men's work, being more seasonal, they did play a more important role in the income provision for the household than the women of the community sample. They also were drawn predominantly from younger, nonlandholding families, so that wage labor was more critical to subsistence.

We have also seen that relatives play an important role in helping some families. About a fifth of the community sample, but only a small percentage of the workers, were receiving financial help from this source.

6 Housing, Housing Tenancy, and Loan Taking

One question that this research addresses is whether the women who work for wages can be said to be better off in terms of current living conditions, resources, and so forth. This question is not easy to answer, because the working women may have come from a background of greater need than many of the nonworkers, many of whom have land assets. Showing a difference, furthermore, does not mean that the difference was caused by the difference in worker status. However, there are a few comparisons that can be suggestive. The first has to do with housing. With some money, one can move to a better house or repair one's present house. If the workers are able to increase their household spending because of their earnings, one type of expenditure might be for improved housing.

HOUSING TYPE

In this section the data relating to housing characteristics are presented, first for the community sample, then for the worker sample. A general question is whether the worker group will tend to have better housing than the other, due to the greater availability to the woman of income to spend on housing and housing improvements.

The respondents were classified in terms of four measures of housing type, according to the predominant materials in the walls and floors, as well as the presence or absence of electricity and running water. The basic results are shown in Tables 6.1 and 6.2. In the community sample, the predominant wall type was *palma*, a board made from the split trunk of a palm tree. Almost as common were wood and concrete, with a few houses built of zinc (tin), and a few of more primitive construction (*yagua* and *tejamanil* houses are basically put together from "sticks" of hardwood or from broad, dried leaves of the *yagua* plant over a frame, but they do not give much protection against the elements). In addition, there were eight houses in the sample of carton, discarded materials, and/or whatever the people could pick up that might make part of a wall.

Of these types, the best construction is of reinforced concrete block, which was found in a fourth of the homes. These are followed in quality by wood, zinc, and *palma*, which made up the bulk of wall types (about two-thirds). The less desirable materials (*tejamanil*, cartons, discards) were used in about 8 percent of the houses in the sample.

The worker sample homes were hardly different, with 27 percent being of reinforced concrete block (compared with 25 percent). However, only two of the houses were of least desirable construction, "cast-offs."

In looking at floor types, the community sample has a predominance of cement floors (71.8 percent), with a fourth (25.5 percent) having only dirt floors. Two of the houses in this sample had "granite" or terrazzo floors, the predominant floor type in middle-class urban homes.

In comparing this group with the worker sample, the workers seem to be slightly better off on the average. Only 19 percent of workers' homes had dirt floors, with 77 percent being of concrete construction and one of terrazzo. Though the differences are slight, they are in the expected direction, favoring the worker group.

Some 62.4 percent of the community sample families had electricity in the house, and 49.6 percent had running water. Thus, electricity is more common than water in the house, with about half of the houses without the latter. When compared with the community sample, the workers are equally likely to have electricity (61.4 percent have it) and water in the house (50.0 percent have running water). Thus, on these measures, no differences appear. I was told that whether one has electricity or water is more a function of which village one lives in than of one's economic situation, as some villages have received electricity while others have not. If this is so, then these last measures are not good indicators of level of living.

Table 6.1
Predominant Wall Construction of House, by
Sample (percentages)

Wall type	Community sample	Worker sample
Reinforced concrete	25.2	27.1
Wood	28.7	37.1
Palma	31.3	24.3
Zinc (tin)	6.1	4.3
Yagua, tejamanil	1.7	4.3
Carton, castoffs	7.0	2.9
Total	100.0	100.0
(n)	(115)	(70)

Table 6.2
Floor Type of House, by Sample (percentages)

Floor type	Community sample	Worker sample
Mosaic, granite, terrazzo	1.8	1.5
Wood	0.0	2.9
Cement	71.8	76.5
Dirt	25.5	19.1
Total	100.0	100.0
(n)	(109)	(68)

TENANCY OF HOUSING

The respondents were also asked whether they owned, rented, or were living in a freely ceded house. Of the community sample, 24 percent were renting, while 74 percent owned (or were buying) their house. Of the workers, a similar percentage (70 percent) were owners, with 26 percent being renters. Thus, overall, no real differences between the two groups are apparent on this measure as well. Again, however, this may not be a good indicator of economic status, as the "ownership" of houses seems to be informally decided, except for better houses.

LOANS

Respondents were asked if anyone in the family had borrowed money in the past year. The assumption was that those under greater stress would have been more likely to have to borrow money, and thus taking a loan would be a sign of lower economic level.

The results show almost no difference between the two samples. About 24 percent of the community sample families borrowed money, as did 21 percent of the worker families. The loans of the community sample families were slightly more likely to have been paid back (69 percent versus 61 percent), but the difference is too small to be important.

CONCLUSION

Overall, not much can be said at this point about differences in basic level of living. Such differences as may exist appear to be small. The best indicators of housing quality--type of wall construction and type of floor--show a slight advantage for the workers. This is primarily because very few of them were living in the worst type of housing, compared with the community sample, but in general there was great similarity between the groups on this measure. The most important finding here is that about a fourth of all households in these villages have only dirt floors, a third are without electricity, and half have no inside plumbing. Most of the poorer households have none of these.

Family, Marital Status,
and Attitudes

The family and marital characteristics of the women in this study are of interest because of our lack of previous knowledge about the traditional Dominican family, and because moving from traditional home-based roles to wage labor often has implications for marital roles and stability. In this chapter, we will describe selected family characteristics of the women in both samples, including their current marital status and marital history.

THE DOMINICAN FAMILY

There are few descriptions in print about the Dominican family. Those which exist are often based not on careful empirical observations but on stereotypes, myth, and cultural ideals that may not be widely practiced. In one of the most recent discussions of the Dominican family, Cross-Beras (1980) pointed out the lack of availability of data on the family and called for research on the topic. One of the most thorough of the traditional descriptions is that of Weil (1973) in the *Area Handbook*.

Weil (1973) opens his description of family and kinship in the Dominican Republic with the cliche "The family is still the most important social unit." This kind of statement can be misleading, implying that families have an important determining influence on other institutions. Most recent sociological theories of family structure, by contrast, tend to see families as largely defined and limited by the more important institutions of economy, polity, and patriarchy.

Among characteristics ascribed to the Dominican family by Weil and others are (1) the predominance of consensual unions in the lower classes; (2) the importance of the institution of *compadrazgo* (godparenting), a "vital institution at every societal level"; (3) traditional values of solidarity, honor, and parental authority among the elites, less held among the lower classes; (4) an ideal of patriarchy, with strong sibling ties among brothers; (5) strong emphasis on extended kin relationships.

In the lower classes, according to Weil, there is less stability of marriage, with a consequent loss of male authority, and the growth of three-generation matrilineal families. Weil also claims that male children are more highly valued than female children, and that large families are desired to reflect the father's virility and to provide greater security for the parents in old age. He also asserts that the "legal, church marriage is accepted by all as more respectable and desirable, but those in the lower classes do not usually live up to this ideal." Weil argues that women "settle for consensual union because of their low socioeconomic position and lack of bargaining power."

In terms of male and female roles, Weil (1973:74-75) states that for males the ideal of machismo is important. This concept involves virility, daring, forcefulness, competitiveness, drama, heroism, and sexual prowess. For the lower-class male, the emphasis is on sexual prowess; he proves his manhood by sexual conquest. Thus men may have more than one family, and this increases their masculine pride.

For the female, the ideal is said to be passivity and gentleness (Weil 1973:74-75). She derives her status from her husband, and dedicates her energy to creating a comfortable home for him and the children. For lower-class females, work outside the home may be necessary. Weil mentions the sexual double standard, in which wives are expected to be faithful to their husbands while husbands are free to engage in sexual relations with other women with impunity. Most of Weil's points are echoed by Cross-Beras (1980).

In this chapter and later ones, we will examine evidence that will allow us to evaluate the descriptions of the lower-class Dominican family by Weil and Cross-Beras. One important difference between the present study and theirs is that the findings of this study are based on carefully carried out interviews--that is, on empirical data instead of common beliefs. The other crucial difference is that the present study is based on interviews with women: in their homes, not in the presence of their husbands, and carried out by women of similar backgrounds. Thus, the present study is very important in providing a much-needed look at these questions from the point of view of women, not of men. Such a view has not been available before.

FAMILY TYPE AND MARITAL HISTORY

Some 80 percent of the principal families of the community households consisted of nuclear families: a father, a mother, and their children. Only 16 percent were mother-child households, and only two were couples without children. In the worker sample, by contrast, a smaller proportion of families were complete nuclear families (63 percent), and relatively more were mother-child households (31.4 percent).

Similar differences can be seen in the comparison of current marital status (Table 7.1). The community sample included 83.7 percent in marriage or union, with 10 percent divorced or separated, and 6 percent widowed. The worker group had fewer women in union or marriage (70 percent), and relatively more who were divorced or separated. All of the women in both samples had been married or in a union at some time in the past, but the workers were more likely to be currently without a husband.

The data in Table 7.1 also show a difference in the two groups in the tendency to marry legally. While only two members (4.3 percent) of the worker sample were married, 13 percent of the community sample were. Of the 98 community women currently in marital unions, 15 percent were legally married, compared with 7 percent of the women in the worker sample. Even for the community sample, the percentage of legal marriages was low compared with the country as a whole, where the ratio of "concubinage" to legal marriage is about 1.6 (from Baez 1986:22). This ratio for our community sample was 5.5 free unions for each legal marriage, and for the worker sample, 15 to 1. Thus, the community women were about three times as likely to be in legal marriages as those in the worker sample; furthermore, the workers were almost three times as likely to be divorced or separated.

The two samples were also compared on marital history, in terms of the number of unions they had had and the number of divorces, if any. Workers were more likely to have experienced multiple unions. Some 25 percent of the

Table 7.1
Current Marital Status of Respondent, by Sample
(percentages)

Marital status	Community sample	Worker sample
Free union	70.9	65.7
Married	12.8	4.3
Divorced/separated	10.3	28.6
Widowed	6.0	1.4
Total	100.0	100.0
(n)	(117)	(70)

community women had experienced more than one union, and a few, more than two. By comparison, about 36 percent of workers had had more than one union, and 10 percent, more than two. (Table 7.2).

The data on divorce history show even more clearly the difference between the two samples. Of the members of the worker sample, half had been divorced or separated at some time, compared with 31 percent of the community sample. Moreover, of those having been divorced in the worker group, the majority (22 of 35) had been divorced or separated more than once. Since this group is, on the average, younger than the community group, this difference is even more striking, since they have not had as much time as the others to experience multiple unions. Because of their younger age and their greater experience of divorce, the average length of the current marriage was much shorter for the worker group: the median for them was 7 years, compared with 18 years for the married/united women in the community sample.

Thus, we see some evidence of lesser marital stability among the women in the worker sample. Perhaps they resemble those Dominican women to whom Brown (1975) referred as having a "multiple-mate" pattern as one strategy of survival in poverty. Perhaps their working leads to a greater tendency to end an unsatisfactory relationship, since with her own source of income a woman is less dependent on a man. When a woman works for wages, this change from traditional roles is also likely to demand some adjustments in

Table 7.2
Marital History of Respondents, by Sample (percentages)

A. Number of unions ever experienced:	Community sample	Worker sample
One	75.9	64.3
Two	19.0	25.0
Three or more	5.2	10.7
Total	100.1	100.0
(n)	(116)	(28)

B. Number of separations or divorces:	Community sample	Worker sample
None	69.0	49.3
One	22.4	18.8
Two or more	8.6	31.9
Total	100.0	100.0
(n)	(116)	(69)

the home, and it might at times fly in the face of expectations that spouses have of one another, thus increasing tensions if adjustments are not made. There is ample evidence from other countries that these kinds of processes can follow women's movement into the wage-labor force (Bane 1976).

However, we cannot know for sure, at this point, whether the noted difference in marital stability is an effect, or a cause, of the status of women as workers outside the home. It is just as reasonable to assume that those women with the least commitment to traditional roles would be more likely than others to seek employment outside the home. The same applies to women with greater family responsibilities, including divorced or separated women. The truth is probably that greater marital instability is both cause and effect of employment. A cause, because it motivates the woman to seek ways to survive and the employment provides an opportunity to this end. And an effect, because a husband who does not contribute to the family's income, or who spends money on his personal needs, may come to be seen as a drain on the family's resources rather than as a source of support. The woman, because of her ability to support herself and her children without the help of the husband, may opt for divorce if she believes the marriage is a poor one or that her husband is draining the family's resources. She has this option, which traditional women did not have, because of her wage-earning abilities.

WORK AND MARITAL CONFLICT

There is some evidence that the fact that some of these women work is a source of conflict at home with their *maridos*. In a subsample of 41 workers, the respondents were asked directly what their husbands thought of their working: if they opposed or supported it. In addition, they were asked if their working had caused any problems, either with their husbands or within the family.

Over half of the 30 married respondents in this subsample said that their husbands supported them or did not oppose their working (56.7 percent). However, a sizable minority--43.3 percent--said their husbands did not like their working. Some of the women reported serious disagreements with their husbands over this issue.

For example, 6 of 29 respondents said that their work had caused fighting, arguments, and even separations from the husband. Another reported that her husband complains because he has to take care of the children while she works. (This was one of the very few cases in which a husband cares for the children while the wife works.) For the majority, however, no problems were mentioned. The only other type of problem, mentioned more often by single mothers, was the inability to get the housework done and take care of the children when one works.

It is possible, then, that increased conflicts arise from a woman's work. However, most of these women were determined to continue working in spite of the husband's complaints, "for the children" or in order to pay the bills. These women gave their economic contribution to the family precedence over the traditional norm of pleasing one's husband.

The women were also asked to evaluate their current unions, according to the question "Do you think your current marriage or union is better or worse than you expected?"

About half of the women in both samples said that their current unions were better than they had expected, and another 28 percent of the community sample expressed general satisfaction with their marriages. The worker sample was more likely to express dissatisfaction, with 31.2 percent either saying their marriages were definitely worse than expected or expressing general dissatisfaction (compared with 19 percent of the community sample). There is more similarity between the two samples on this question than there is difference, with the majority of both samples being fairly satisfied with their unions. This does not necessarily mean that they are happy in their unions, but they do not seem to see them as worse than their expectations.

ATTITUDES ABOUT MARRIAGE

We have seen that the two samples differ somewhat in actual marital experience. It is of interest to see if they also differ in their attitudes or beliefs about marriage and its meaning. In this section, data are presented on three aspects of those attitudes: whether formal marriage is preferred to the *union libre*, and the ideal descriptions of the "good husband" and the "good wife."

All women were asked the question "For a woman in your situation, is it better to marry or just to live with a man in a *union libre*?" The responses to this question show that neither form is greatly preferred over the other in the community sample--about 47 percent chose each response, with the rest saying it did not matter. The responses of the worker sample leaned more toward the *union libre*, with 61 percent preferring that form and 36 percent preferring marriage.

These data also reveal some discrepancy between the ideal and the practical level, since in fact the free union is much more common than marriage. Thus, many of those in free unions actually preferred marriage, while none of those in marriages preferred the *union libre*. These responses reveal, more than anything else, the inability of many women to live up to their ideals. They also show, of course, that the consensual union is an acceptable, or even preferable, choice to a large enough part of the community to not be considered "deviant." This is in contrast with the assertion by Weil (1973) that marriage is overwhelmingly seen as more desirable than the free union.

For those choosing either marriage or free union as a preference, the interviewer asked why. Many of those who chose marriage did so because they believed marriage to be associated with greater responsibility on the part of the man, and more security "or tranquillity" for the wife. A few typical examples:

> "Because the woman feels more tranquil if she's married."

> "It's better to have responsibility in the home, and to have a husband who pays attention to his children."

> "There's more responsibility on the part of the man."

> "One feels more secure with him; he's more responsible."

The factors of responsibility and security were mentioned by about half of the women in the community sample who preferred marriage. In the worker sample there also seems to be a concern, among those who prefer marriage, for the greater responsibility that marriage brings.

Another factor, mentioned by 13 percent of those preferring marriage in the community sample and 15 percent of the corresponding group of workers, was the greater rights that a woman has against a man if she is married. For example, they said such things as

> "Married, there is more respect, more responsibility, and the woman has more claims against the man."

> "With the law you have more rights."

> "There's more support against the man, ..."

A few women also mentioned the greater respect within the community that one has as a woman and as a family if one is married. ("One can go anywhere if one is married.") Very few mentioned religious or moral reasons for their preference for marriage. The great majority of reasons, for both groups of women, had to do with the greater male responsibility associated with marriage, as well as with the legal support for this responsibility.

The members of both samples who preferred the *union libre* to marriage had a more difficult time stating the reasons for their preference. Most of the reasons given center on the failures of marriage, the corruption of men, and the need to be able to terminate poor relationships with ease. Those giving this type of response said such things as

> "It's better to have two single people who love each other than two married people who don't understand each other."

> "Married people have many problems."

> "Well, it's better for me because the people who marry don't stay together. They marry and then they turn around looking for a divorce."

> "This is better, because when one leaves, there aren't any problems with papers."

A number of women gave more positive responses, indicating a desire for more freedom, fewer ties, and fewer "compromises"--although one has the feeling that these responses are mainly defenses against poor expectations with respect to men and marriage. For example, they said

> "It's better if the ties are looser."

> "It's better to live without many obligations to the men of today."

The largest group who preferred the *union libre* cited the faults of men as their reason:

> "Because men are neither good nor faithful, and you can't marry them 'with paper'."

> "Because the men of today are 'without shame' and have many women."

> "Because one suffers much with men."

In other words, for many of the women, their attitude toward marriage was negative, and they were pessimistic about their ability to have good relationships with men. Their suspicions led them to prefer free-union arrangements over marriage, in order to keep their ability to terminate poor relationships and to maintain some control over their lives. Overall, for both those who prefer marriage and those who prefer the free union, there often seems to be a general assumption that men are not to be trusted or depended on, and that at times marriage can improve these characteristics of men, though at times it simply ties the woman down within a difficult situation.

Many of the women also seem to believe that in past generations, men had more responsibility to their families. The "men of today" are said to be "corrupt," irresponsible, and "without shame"; those in the past were better husbands and fathers. It is possible that there is some truth to this belief. In past generations, perhaps social control within small traditional communities was more effective. Men had work on their *parcelas*, and their place in the scheme of things was spelled out in social norms. But with social change, including the loss of the ability to carry out their traditional part in family maintenance, the old norms do not serve as well. Men are often jobless and landless (or nearly so), and have few hopes within these communities of ever improving their situation to any great extent. The women often blame the "irresponsibility" of men rather than the loss of land, lack of jobs, and lack of resources that has resulted from large-scale economic change.

THE "GOOD WIFE" AND THE "GOOD HUSBAND"

The women were asked to give a description of a good wife and a good husband, with the question "Please describe a good (wife/husband). What does (s)he do? What characteristics does (s)he have?" The responses were classified into the categories given in Tables 7.3 and 7.4. By looking at these two tables, one can see something of the expectations these women have for the "ideal" husband or wife, and by comparing the two samples we can see if there are any differences that set the worker group apart from the more traditional group.

For women in the community sample, the most common descriptions of a good wife were that a good woman takes care of her husband and that she is faithful to him. She

Table 7.3
Description of a "Good Wife": Characteristics
Mentioned (percent mentioning each trait)

Traits mentioned	Community sample (n=115)	Worker sample (n=28)
Takes care of husband, attends to his needs	36.5	32.1
Faithful	22.6	21.4
Behaves well with husband, gets along well	19.1	10.7
Respects husband, is kind, considerate, understanding	18.3	46.5
Takes care of children, educates them	17.4	21.4
Responsible, fulfills duties	15.7	0.0
"Woman of the house"	13.9	17.9
Does housework well, cooks, cleans	11.3	17.9
Doesn't "do him wrong"	10.4	14.3
Obeys him, does what he wants	9.6	7.1
Takes interest in home	7.0	14.3
Loves husband, is affectionate	5.2	10.7
"A good wife"	4.3	7.1
Does things well, on time	3.5	0.0
Doesn't fight	2.6	3.6
Helps her companion	2.6	0.0
Is not jealous	1.7	3.6
Other	4.5	7.8

Table 7.4
Description of a "Good Husband": Characteristics
Mentioned (percent mentioning each trait)

Traits mentioned	Community sample (n=108)	Worker sample (n=26)
Provides for the family	49.0	46.2
Doesn't mistreat his wife/children; doesn't fight	21.3	26.9
Responsible; fulfills duties	16.7	7.7
Takes care of wife (family); solves their problems	15.7	7.7
Behaves well with wife, gets along	11.1	7.7
Understanding, kind, serious, considerate, respectful	11.1	42.3
Pays attention to his home	8.3	7.7
Is affectionate, loves wife	8.3	19.2
United; faithful	4.6	3.8
Is not "corrupt"; doesn't spend money in the streets, on rum, on other women	5.5	3.8
Happy, cheerful	3.7	0.0
Educates, helps care for children	2.8	7.7
Shares decisions with wife	0.9	0.0

"behaves herself" with him; is respectful, kind, and considerate; and takes care of her children. In addition, she is a "woman of the house," who stays at home and does not want to go out. She "always is at home in her house." And finally, about 10 percent of the respondents said that a good wife does not "do him wrong" and that she "obeys" her husband. There were a variety of other responses, all listed in the table, but none of these were given by as many as 10 percent of the respondents.

Thus the traditional values of serving the husband and being faithful to him seem to be strong in these responses, as well as the values of being a good mother and a woman of the house (*mujer de la casa*). When we compare these responses with those of the worker group, we see similarity as well as some difference. For the workers, the idea of taking care of (or attending to) the needs of the husband was strong, as was the idea of faithfulness and good parenting. There is some evidence, however, that the worker women are more in tune with a "romantic" or egalitarian conception of marriage (Theodorson 1965), which includes the idea of equality between the spouses, communication, sharing, and love as a basis for marriage. For example, 46.5 percent of these women mentioned that a good wife respects her husband or is kind, considerate, understanding, and so forth, qualities that imply a close personal intimacy in marriage not expected in traditional marriage. Only 18 percent of the community sample mentioned these traits. Also, the workers were less likely to mention such things as responsibility to duty, a more traditional concept. Finally, the workers were slightly more likely to mention traits such as love and taking an interest in the home, although these differences were small. The main differences seem to be in the stronger emphasis on qualities of the interpersonal relationship and less on responsibility to duty among the workers. One could say, then, that their attitudes appear to be less traditional and somewhat more individualistic and concerned with the quality of the relationship in marriage.

When asked to describe a good husband, the most common type of response for both samples, mentioned by almost half of each group, was that a good husband is a provider for his family--he spends what he earns on the family's needs and not just on himself; he gives money to his wife for the family's needs; and he tries to find work in order to be able to provide for the family. Next in importance was that a good husband does not mistreat his wife, does not fight with her, is not aggressive, and so forth. Also of some importance to the community sample women were responsibility to duty and "taking care" of the family. About 11 percent of this sample also mentioned each of the following as traits of a good husband: that he behaves well with his wife, that he is understanding, kind, considerate, and/or respectful, and that he pays attention to his home.

Thus, the idea of a good husband differs from that of a good wife in that husbands ideally are expected to play a more instrumental role (the provider role), while wives are to attend to their husbands' needs at home. There is more emphasis on the idea that a good husband should not mistreat or hit his wife than the other way around, probably because husband-to-wife aggression is much more common than wife-to-husband aggression. The idea that a husband should be faithful, moreover, is relatively uncommon, mentioned by only about 5 percent of these respondents, in comparison with its relative importance for wives.

Thus, through these responses we see evidence of the persistence of the traditional double standard and dual role expectations for men and women in marriage. The provider role of the husband is emphasized, and there is a relative absence of concern with his parental role, contribution to household duties, or faithfulness. For the wife, by contrast, faithfulness and attention to the needs of the husband are primary, and her mother role is also seen as important. In the pattern of answers, one also sees a clear strain of patriarchy or male dominance--the wife is to serve the husband, obey him, cook for him, and so forth, but he is expected to solve the family's problems and give his wife what she needs for the family. For him, there is no mention of anything close to obedience. One has the impression that as long as he is not aggressive and gives his wife enough money for household subsistence, a man is considered to be a good husband, regardless of his other traits.

When we compare the responses of the worker sample with those of the other women, we find some of the same types of differences that were noted in the discussion of the "good wife." Specifically, the workers are less concerned with duty and responsibility, and they are much more concerned with the qualitative aspects of the relationship. They were almost four times as likely to want a husband who was understanding, kind, considerate, and/or respectful as were the traditional women. In addition, workers were more likely to mention love and affection as important qualities in a husband. In fact, traits such as understanding and respect were almost as commonly mentioned as the "good provider" traits by the workers. Again, there is evidence that the attitudes of the women workers reflect a more individualistic or "romantic" conception of marriage, which includes an emphasis on the quality of the interpersonal relationship and not so much just the fulfillment of the traditional obligations of marriage.

After describing the "ideal" husband, respondents were asked to evaluate the reality of husbands against this backdrop of the ideal. First, they were asked, "Are many men like that?" To this, 44.6 percent of the responses of the community sample were positive, with over half being "No." The women in the worker sample were even less positive, with only 31.3 percent answering "Yes." In other words, most women thought that most men were not like their description of the good husband.

Then the women were asked to describe the "typical" husband in their community. Of 91 women in the community sample responding to this question, half (51.6 percent) gave negative descriptions, which included the following traits: "They drink too much"; "they're *machista*"; "they're corrupt"; "they're gamblers"; "they don't give much to their wives"; and "they don't like to work." Only 34 percent of the community sample gave positive descriptions ("good"; "hard workers"), and the others gave either neutral responses or both positive and negative responses.

The worker women were slightly less positive, as 50 percent gave a definitely negative response; 19.2 percent, a positive response; and 30.8 percent neutral or positive and negative responses. Thus, the workers were less likely to believe that most men were like their descriptions of good husbands, and they were less likely to describe the typical husband of their community wholly in positive terms. Even though the women in the community sample were more likely to be positive, however, the majority of them were negative in their assessments of the men of the community.

Perhaps the difference between the two groups is related to the fact that the workers were more likely to have been divorced, which probably means that their actual experience with the men of the community had been more negative. The similarities again seem to outweigh the differences, however, as in both groups the sense of disaffection with men appears to be high.

SUMMARY AND CONCLUSION

We have seen that the women in the worker sample were more likely than others to have been divorced, to have had multiple unions, and to be currently divorced or separated. The workers were somewhat more likely to prefer the free union over legal marriage, and they were much less likely to be legally married than were the nonworkers. There was not much difference in their level of satisfaction with their current unions/marriages.

In their explanations as to why they preferred marriage or the *union libre*, the workers' responses seemed to indicate less concern with "security" and more with freedom, ease of ending a poor relationship, and independence. In addition, in their descriptions of the ideal husband and wife, the worker group expressed greater concern about interpersonal aspects of marriage and less about "duty." In general, their attitude toward men in the community was less positive than the attitude of the community sample.

Although the direction of causality among working, attitudes, marital status, and divorce experience is not clear, there is reason to believe that the traditional family structure may change to some extent when women take outside wage labor, especially when their husbands are unemployed. Similar findings have been reported in other studies of women's employment in similar contexts (Safa 1986:66). Even in countries such as the United States, the employment of women outside the home is associated with higher divorce rates (see, for example, Bane 1976). But the lack of marital stability in itself may not necessarily be negative. The earnings of the woman give her a degree of independence that she did not have before. If, therefore, she is in an intolerable relationship with her husband, she can end the relationship and still hope to support herself and her children. This is not an option for the traditional woman. We do see that the intact marriages in the worker group are not any less satisfactory than those in the community sample. It is possible that the tolerance level for negative behaviors of husbands (described by both groups in the responses about the "typical" husband) is lower for the worker group, because they are not so dependent on the union for survival.

The other side of this association between marital separation and worker status, of course, is that women who are separated or divorced must find ways of supporting themselves and their families, and thus they will have a greater likelihood of seeking outside employment. Another possible factor is that, given traditional values about woman's "place," married women who would like to work for wages may face resistance from their husbands, who do not want "their wives" working away from the house. This, also, would increase the percentage of separated or divorced women in the worker group, relative to in-union or married women.

The workers also seem to be somewhat more independent in their attitudes toward marriage and in their conceptions of the "good husband" and "good wife." They are more interested in the quality of the relationship between spouses than are the nonworkers, who focus primarily on the husband's economic contributions.

We might surmise that working for wages increases a woman's resources, which gives her a degree of independence and greater self-reliance, which can in turn disrupt traditional roles in the family, possibly leading to higher divorce/separation rates, more negative attitudes toward men, and higher expectations for husbands. The ideal husband is no longer the man who supports the family, but the man who is willing to share in the support of the family and to be a good companion as well.

The greater independence and the greater tendency to be the household head, then, further motivate the women to work, to continue working, and to move even further from the traditional role as woman "of the house."

8 Marital Resource Sharing and Decision Making

One of the concerns of development research in recent years has been the degree to which women and children are included in income improvements brought about by economic development. This is partly a function of the way in which resources customarily are divided within the household. For example, in some societies, money earned by men is not used for household needs, since those needs are the responsibility of women (Boserup 1970). Furthermore, where men are expected to support their families with the provision of money, food, or other necessities, there can be negative impacts of development strategies that are oriented primarily toward men. It has often been found that where women are left out of income-generating opportunities while men are included, changes occur in the balance of power and resource control within the household, to the detriment of women (see, for example, Flora and Santos 1986; Safa 1986). On the other hand, studies have found that when women gain economic resources through entrepreneurial activities or through employment for wages, their position within the community and family may be improved, and patriarchal norms may begin to break down (Lim 1983:83; Abraham-Van der Mark 1983; Moses 1977).

In this chapter, we will try to assess the effects of women's paid labor outside the home on family resource division and, especially, on decision making and control of expenditures within the household. Not much is known about such matters from previous research (Safa 1986).

RESOURCE DIVISION

The women in this survey were asked two questions that focus directly on resource division. The first was "Does your husband give you enough money for the needs of the family?" (and if not, why not?). In response to this, about half of the women of each sample said "yes." However, of married women only, two-thirds of the community sample and 58 percent of the worker sample responded "yes." Thus, the majority of married women felt that their husbands gave them an amount "sufficient" for the needs of the family.

For those who responded negatively, about two-thirds of the women gave as reasons the husbands' lack of work or lack of sufficient earnings to cover the family's needs. The other third gave responses that suggested that the husband did not share his income with the family, but instead spent it "on other women," "in the streets," or in ways unknown to the wife. Of course, this is only a small percentage (about 13 percent) of all wives in the sample, but it is a considerable portion of those who do not feel they receive enough from their husbands' incomes.

A second question asked the women was "Who keeps the family's money?" This is in part a measure of power, since the person who keeps the money can often make decisions about how it is spent. It is assumed that in those families in which the wife keeps the money (or part of it), she has more access to its use than in families in which the husband alone keeps the family's money.

Table 8.1 shows the responses to this question for both samples. In most cases, the respondent kept the family's money, although this was more common in the worker group. A large difference can be seen in the likelihood that only the husband keeps the family's money, with about one-fourth of the community sample in that category and only 7.5 percent of the workers. Even if we compare only married respondents, we find that 27.6 percent of the married respondents of the community sample say that their husbands keep the family's money, compared with only 10 percent of the workers. Given the strong gender-based division of labor (to be discussed later) in the home, and the fact that purchases of household goods, food, and clothing are made by women, this fact could be associated with a lesser ability of the women in the community sample to make purchases adequate for the family's needs. Thus, although wives in both samples were the most frequent money keepers, this tendency was less frequent in the community sample. Those husbands

Table 8.1
Who Keeps the Family's Money?   (percentages)

Who keeps money?	Community sample	Worker sample
Respondent	56.9	74.6
Husband	24.8	7.5
Both; each his own	13.8	10.4
Bank	1.8	0.0
Other	2.8	7.5
Total	100.1	100.0
(n)	(109)	(67)

who do keep the money have greater potential to control its use.

DECISION MAKING AND CONTROL OF SPENDING

Respondents were asked who in the household made decisions about various household needs. Measuring marital (and household) power by means of asking about decision making is a commonly used technique in sociology, pioneered by Blood and Wolfe (1960). In the present context, we are interested in the extent to which women are making decisions, and in what areas of decision making they have more power. Finally, we will be interested to see if the decision-making power of the working women is greater than, or different from, that of their more traditional sisters. This pertains to the general question of whether women's status within families changes as a result of their wage-labor work. There is some reason to expect that increased monetary contribution to the family brings increased power to make decisions about how money is spent, as well as improved status in general.

Tancer (1973) wrote that the dominance of the male in the traditional lower-class rural household "is more apparent than real" (1973:214). This was so, she argued, because women have the responsibility for running the household, tending the children, and so forth, while men stay out of these matters. This type of argument is misleading, based on an unrealistic notion of power. Power, or lack of power, is the result of several factors. If one's alternatives are limited to none, then one may act out one's role without obvious coercion but still be powerless because there is no possibility of free choice of roles. Furthermore, resources are an important source of power--if one has no resources with which to carry out one's plans or wishes, one is powerless. A woman might "run a household" not out of free choice but out of a lack of any other alternative, and certainly this is not against the wishes of her husband. If he were to decide that she should no longer cook *pollo*, and she continues to cook *pollo*, then she is exercising some power. But if she carries out her role within the confines of what is expected or desired by the culture and her husband, then she does not necessarily have power.

Finally, if a woman is dependent on her husband for survival, if he controls the resources necessary for her to carry out her role, then she is in a powerless position relative to him. Her control over the kitchen is limited by his control over the money for food purchases. Recent work in the sociology of the family has demonstrated the critical connection between family power and control over resources. Thus, where women have few resources, where they depend on men to provide their necessities, they are not really possessors of power even though they may "run the household." They do this within the range of leeway allowed them by their husbands, who control the family resources. The woman may "choose" what to cook, for example, but she does this at least partly to please her husband (or to avoid displeasing him). It is because of these considerations that, in studying power relationships in the household, we look at both who "makes decisions" and who "controls expenditures" for carrying out those decisions. Only if the woman does both can she be said to have control over an activity. Decision making without the ability to carry out the decision is not power.

Respondents were first asked a general question, "Who decides how to spend money in your family?" The responses to this question are shown in Table 8.2. In both samples, the women reported themselves to be the decision makers about spending more than any other person. Thus, 46 percent of the community sample respondents said that they decided how to spend money in their families. In 27 percent of the cases, these decisions were shared with the husband, and in 22 percent, the husband alone reportedly made these

Table 8.2
Who Decides How to Spend Money?   (percentages)

Who decides?	Community sample	Worker sample
Respondent	46.2	75.4
Husband	22.2	8.7
Both	27.4	7.2
Other	4.3	8.7
Total	100.1	100.0
(n)	(117)	(69)

decisions.   Considering only married respondents in the community sample, husbands alone made the decision in 27 percent of the cases, and the women either made the decision or participated in the decision in 60.4 percent of the families (58 of 96 households with husbands).

By comparison, the workers had more decision-making power over spending. About three-fourths (75.4 percent) of the respondents said that they alone decided how to spend money and only 7.2 percent shared the decision with a husband.   Again, considering only married or in-union respondents, only about 13 percent reported that they alone made these decisions, and 83 percent reported that they either made the decisions or participated in them. This latter figure is quite a bit larger than the corresponding figure (60 percent) for the community sample. Thus, there is evidence here that the workers have more control over spending money, partly because of being more likely to head households but also because of being less likely to share decision making about spending with husbands.

Respondents were then asked to say "who decides" and "who controls" expenditures for a list of household needs, shown in Table 8.3.   In that table, the percent of cases in which the respondent reported making each type of decision alone, as well as controlling expenditures for each one alone, is given. In each case, some respondents reported making the decision alone, others said their husbands made the decision, others said they both made the decision, and a few reported other household members as decision makers. However, for

Table 8.3
Percent of Cases in Which Respondent Alone "Decides"
and "Controls" Expenditures for Various
Household Needs, by Sample

Expenditures for	Community sample		Worker sample	
	Woman decides	Woman controls	Woman decides	Woman controls
Food	82.1	58.1	69.0	72.4
Clothes	63.2	43.6	69.0	72.4
Education	52.1	35.9	51.7	58.6
Medicine	49.6	36.8	62.1	51.7
House repairs	29.9	24.8	51.7	51.7
Work implements	8.5	12.0	24.1	24.1
Household goods	50.4	38.5	51.7	51.7
Rent	20.5	12.8	44.8	34.8

most of these household expenses, decisions were mainly made either by the respondent or by her husband, and in some cases the response was that no one makes the decision because there are no such expenditures. Similarly, "control" of spending for each item was usually attributed to either the wife or the husband. Thus, in Table 8.3, only the percentages of decisions and control of expenditures attributed to the respondent are given, since these tend to vary inversely with husbands' input.

In analyzing the responses, some interesting patterns emerge. First, in matters of the traditionally feminine sphere (buying food, household goods, and clothes), the women of the community sample reported that they made the decisions to buy in the majority of households. In addition, women usually claimed to be the sole decision maker in purchases of medicines and expenditures on education, and they were fairly often involved as decision maker for house repair expenses and rent as well. However, the women in the community sample were significantly less likely to "control" the money for the expenditures in all of these areas than to "decide" that money needed to be spent. For example, although the decision about clothes buying was theirs in 63 percent of the cases, they were less likely to say that they actually controlled the money for clothes purchases. In these cases, the "drop" from percentage deciding to percentage controlling was associated with an increase in the husband's input. Hence, in only one area, the purchase of food, did the women of the community sample say that they controlled expenditures in a majority of cases. (Their "control" is greater than decision making in one area, the purchase of work implements, but both of these percentages are very low because these purchases are dominated by husbands.) Even so, it should be noted that a fairly substantial proportion of these women reported controlling expenditures on medicines, education, house repairs, household goods, clothes, and food. Thus, one cannot say that the women of these communities are totally dominated and controlled by men, as some descriptions of Dominican marriages imply.

When we compare the community sample with the worker group, two differences are immediately apparent. First, the workers are more likely to report decision making in almost all areas, including non-"female" areas such as rent payment, work implement purchase, and house repairs. Second, and more important, the percentages for "control" of expenditures for the workers are usually almost as great as their percentages of decision making within a particular area. This is especially interesting, since for the nonworker sample, control was usually quite a bit lower than decision making. This means that the worker group seems to have more control over the family expenditures--they do not "lose" control over actual purchasing to their husbands, as seems to happen in the other sample, even though about two-thirds of them have husbands. More detailed analysis shows that the working women were over ten times as likely to control food and clothing expenditures as their husbands, compared with less than twice as likely for the community sample. In every type of expenditure, workers were more likely to control it than their husbands, but this was not the case for the community women. Thus, the evidence seems to support the idea that outside income tends to increase a woman's status and power within the family, allowing her more control over decisions and expenditures that affect her life.

Finally, two other questionnaire items dealt with decision making or power. Both show similar results when the two samples are compared. First, respondents were asked, "Who makes the decision to borrow money?" For the community sample, 64 percent of those reporting having taken loans said the decision was made by the husband alone, compared with 35 percent of the worker sample; 44 percent of the workers said that they themselves made this decision, compared with only 17 percent of the community women.

The other question was "Who decides about the education of the children?" This question is broader than the one concerning expenditures for education. Here, the question implies decisions about who should go to school and for how many years. Responses are shown in Table 8.4. For both samples, the women were most likely to say they made such decisions themselves, although, as before, the workers had a much higher percentage in that category. Only in about 29 percent of the community sample households with children did the husband alone make those decisions, while in a fourth of households the husband and wife shared the decisions. The workers were less likely to share the decision or to have the decision made by the husband alone, with about 16 percent in each of those categories. Again we see some indication that employment is associated with greater control or power within the household for the women in this study.

Table 8.4
Who Decides About the Children's Education?
(percentages)

Decision maker	Community sample	Worker sample
Respondent	42.4	62.9
Husband	29.3	16.1
Both	25.2	16.1
Other	3.0	4.8
Total	99.9	99.9
(n)	(99)	(62)

SUMMARY

In this chapter we have seen some important differences between the worker sample and the community sample in measures of power and control over resources. In every case, the worker group appeared to have a greater likelihood of decision-making and resource control. For example, they were more likely to keep the family's money and to say that their husband gave them enough money for the family's needs. In areas of decision making, women of both samples had considerable decision-making power and control over expenditures. However, these characteristics were more common among the worker group. In every decision-making comparison, the workers came out ahead of the community sample respondents. Thus, there seems to be clear evidence of improvements in women's position within their households as a result of their income-producing labor.

9   Division of Labor: Women's Work in Agriculture and in the Household

One of the questions that has interested scholars and practitioners involved in economic development efforts is the role of women in traditional agriculture. In some regions, this role has been a dominant one, with women controlling and producing the most important products. In others, women's participation in the actual agricultural activities related to crop production has been minimal, although even in those cases they have important roles, often providing such services as cooking for the laborers, processing products, caring for animals, and generally maintaining the household so that men are free to do the other work.

WOMEN AND AGRICULTURE IN THE DOMINICAN REPUBLIC

In the Dominican Republic, women have not been thought to be much involved in agricultural activities. The roles of men and women are often described as extremely segregated in the rural areas, with men taking most of the roles that require work away from the house. Women, it is often said, are "of the house," and should carry out their work within its limits. The man "does not view his role as helping in the care of the house or children. He leaves that to the woman" (Tancer 1973: 214).

As recently as 1980 (Cross-Beras 1980:279), women in rural agricultural households in the Dominican Republic were described by a sociologist as "passive" and "unproductive," basically housekeepers and child rearers (hardly unproductive activities!). Yet, even before that, there were some who described more extensive roles for rural women. Tancer (1973:214) had written that women were often expected to help with sowing, harvesting, or other activities when the men needed extra hands. She also noted that women did the important task of water carrying, which often meant several miles of walking each day to the nearest water source.

Two more recent studies have addressed this question for the Dominican Republic. In a discussion of an agroforestry project in the central mountains, women's traditional participation in agriculture is described as follows:

> Women share with men the harvesting of annual crops and the coffee harvest (as owners and/or as hired workers). Women raise the small animals (hogs and chickens) for meat and egg production, they usually milk the cows (for home consumption) and they tend patio (door yard) gardens with vegetables, bananas and herbs. Responsibility for fuelwood- and water-gathering falls mostly on the women, with some help from the children. (Fortmann and Rocheleau, 1984:5-6)

The authors go on to describe other productive activities of women in these areas, including cheese, candy, and cassava processing and weaving of palm-fiber containers and chair seats and backs. Similar descriptions of women's activities in the same region were given by Flora and Santos (1986), who emphasize women's craft work, small animal care, gardening, and grain culture. They state that when women perform these activities, they are not usually labeled "agricultural," because "women are not supposed to engage in agriculture" (1986:222).

Similar points are made by Arango (1985), who concludes that Dominican rural women tend to be involved in aspects of agriculture that allow them to combine those tasks with domestic work, that do not require a great deal of physical strength or technical skills, and that involve large numbers of workers, so that available males are often inadequate to the task (for example, the harvest).

Clearly, these women are participants in agriculture as well as other economic activities. They are not "passive" or "nonproductive," as they have been described in other places.

Rather, they are engaged in productive work that is critical to the survival and well being of their families.

The studies just cited focused on the fertile Cibao Valley, the most prosperous agricultural area in the Dominican Republic. It is of interest to investigate the same questions for our respondents, who live in the much less prosperous region near Azua.

With these points in mind, we return to our survey data. We will focus primarily on the community sample for this part of the analysis, since the workers were not representative of "traditional" roles.

AZUA WOMEN AND AGRICULTURE

The women in the Azua study were asked if they worked on the family's farm (*parcela*). Only 16 of the 117 community women (13.7 percent) answered in the affirmative. However, of the 66 women in families who cultivated land, 22.7 percent reported working on the family's farm. While this is a minority, it is a sizable minority, larger than traditional descriptions would lead us to expect.

These women were then asked what kinds of work they did on the farm, beginning with the most important. The most common response was "sowing or planting," which was mentioned by 10 of the 16 women. Other activities mentioned included caring for animals, milking cows, weeding, picking melons or corn, and helping with irrigation. None of these activities, however, was mentioned by more than two or three women. Thus, of women in families practicing crop cultivation, about 15 percent were involved in planting, with a few others reporting other, varied activities.

Another set of questions dealt with the involvement of the women in specific types of farming activities. The interviewer presented a list of activities (care of poultry, care of animals, preparation of land, and so forth) to which the woman was asked to respond by naming the person in the family who is the "principal" performer of that activity, as well as the main "helper," if any. From these data (Table 9.1), one can see that 25 percent of the 117 women of the community sample were involved in the care of poultry. In fact, the woman of the house was the most common "principal" poultry caretaker. In those families with poultry, the respondent was the principal caretaker in 47.5 percent of the cases. In addition, some women reported "helping" in this task, even though they were not the principal person. In all, 75 percent

Table 9.1
Comparison of the Agricultural Activities of Women
and Their Husbands, by Sample (percent who do each
activity, as principal or helper)

Activities	Community sample		Worker sample	
	Principal	Helper	Principal	Helper
Poultry care				
Woman	25.6	6.8	15.7	4.3
Husband	13.7	2.6	7.1	2.9
Animal care				
Woman	18.8	4.3	10.0	5.7
Husband	20.5	2.6	10.0	1.4
Land preparation				
Woman	0.0	0.0	2.9	1.4
Husband	41.9	0.0	24.3	1.4
Planting				
Woman	0.9	0.0	1.4	0.0
Husband	47.0	0.0	22.9	0.0
Apply chemicals				
Woman	0.9	0.0	1.4	0.0
Husband	39.3	0.0	20.0	1.4
Harvest				
Woman	0.9	0.9	2.9	1.4
Husband	46.2	0.0	24.3	0.0
Sell products				
Woman	0.9	0.9	2.9	1.4
Husband	38.5	1.7	22.9	1.4

of the families with poultry had a woman (the respondent, her mother, or another female relative) as either the principal caretaker or as helper. Thus, the care of poultry is quite frequently defined as "woman's" work in these communities.

The care of animals (principally cows and goats) was another task given in the checklist of activities. About 19 percent of the women in the community survey said they were the principal animal caretaker, with another 4 percent acting as helpers (Table 9.1). Of the 60 families who actually kept animals, 22 (36.7 percent) had the respondent as the principal caretaker. In another 5 percent, the respondent was a helper. Women were about as likely as men to be principal animal caretakers (in 40 percent of these cases, the husband was the principal animal caretaker). However, if the principal caretaker was neither the woman nor her husband, it was most likely to be a son (18 percent of households) and never a daughter. As helpers in the care of animals, sons also outnumbered daughters by a 17 to 1 margin. From these data it would appear that caring for animals is often a woman's job but almost never a girl's job.

In the same series of items, respondents were asked to name the principal performer as well as the main helper in the following other tasks: land preparation, planting, application of herbicides, fertilizers, and other chemicals, harvesting crops, and selling the products of the farm. In none of these activities were the women of the community sample reportedly involved to any significant extent, and only rarely were daughters involved. For each activity, usually only one, if any, of the 117 women reported that she was the principal task performer, and at most one other woman was a helper. In the great majority of cases, these tasks were performed by husbands and/or sons, with help occasionally provided by paid laborers, also male.

In the earlier question about what types of jobs the woman did on the farm, a number mentioned planting. In this later series, however, only one woman claimed to be the principal planter or the main helper. It seems likely, therefore, that the degree of involvement of these women in planting is very small, and that they do not see themselves as playing significant roles, even though they might occasionally help with this task. The principal planter, and the main helper, were usually male, with women coming in when more hands were needed.

In summary, the women in the community sample were involved in agriculture mainly in the areas of the care of animals and poultry. Both of these tasks can be done close to the house, and so can be combined with the woman's traditional home-based duties. In addition, some women helped occasionally with planting, and a very few others were involved in other tasks, such as weeding or the harvest.

Thus far we have dealt only with the results for the women in the community sample. Among the worker sample relatively few families were involved in agriculture. For example, while about 50 percent of the community sample families had members engaged in the tasks of plowing, planting, harvesting, and keeping animals, only 20-30 percent of the 70 families of the workers were involved in these tasks. In most cases, then, neither the woman nor her husband was involved in these activities. Nonetheless, the general pattern of results shown for the workers in Table 9.1 follows that of the traditional sample, though at lower participation levels. Thus, the most common activities for those women were poultry care and animal care, while husbands dominated the activities related to crop production.

Overall, then, although women's activities in agriculture are somewhat limited, they quite often include the care of animals and poultry. In addition, the woman's role as provider of water, food, fuel, and clothing for the males in the family supports their work in agriculture; without this provision the male activity would be much more difficult, if not impossible. For this reason, perhaps, a few women answered the question "What jobs do you do on the family farm?" with "I make the coffee." To Dominican workers, having their coffee a few times a day is as essential to their task as having the right implements. Thus, the woman's job is deemed an important contribution to the work of the family as a whole.

Compared with the women described in the mountainous regions of the country (Flora and Santos 1986; Fortmann and Rocheleau 1984), the women of Azua appear to have more restricted economic activities. There is very little craft work in this area of the country, and their agricultural work is less varied. These differences are probably due to the arid conditions in Azua. Even men's work here is less productive and less varied than in the greener, less arid Cibao region. The bleak conditions of the Azua Valley put limits not only on everyone's ability to survive but on their range of possible activities as well.

DIVISION OF LABOR IN HOUSEHOLD TASKS

In contrast with the less than universal participation of households in agricultural work, every family has housework--cleaning, cooking, care of clothing, and (usually) child care. The following is a brief description of the main duties carried out by traditional women in the communities in this study, based on my observations.

One time-consuming task done daily is food preparation. It is usually done outside the main house, either in an open-sided, thatched-roof kitchen or in the backyard. This is because cooking is done on an open wood or charcoal fire, which has to be built where smoke can escape. Meal preparation takes a great deal of time. Wood must be brought for the fire. Water is sometimes carried from a stream or an irrigation ditch. Beans must be shelled; plantains must be boiled and peeled; corn must be picked and cleaned. Chickens must be caught, killed, cleaned, and cut up. Even the rice must be washed before cooking. Often women spend the better part of a morning preparing the midday meal, which almost always includes rice and beans. Also common are plantains, usually cut into small pieces and fried in oil. Those who are able also eat meat or chicken, usually fried or cooked in a tomato sauce. The most common meal in these communities is simply rice with a small amount of red beans.

Cleaning the kitchen and house is also a daily chore. Cement floors are usually swept and mopped daily. The yards around the houses are dusty, and the houses have open windows and doors that let in the dust, so that daily cleaning is necessary. Even houses with dirt floors are carefully swept each day, to keep down the dust. Often the front yard is swept. Dishes, cooking implements, and other kitchen items must be washed, usually outside in cold water with a little soap.

Children are cared for as the women go about their chores. Girls are given child-care tasks as soon as they are able to do them--age six or older. By the time children are able to walk, they are out in groups, playing fairly freely in the neighborhood. Boys often go naked until age eight or so in these communities. Girls begin to be dressed, at least in panties, at a much younger age, around two years.

Children get very dirty in this situation, and accidents, burns, and injuries are common. Older children bathe in the irrigation ditches where these are nearby, but in other villages, baths are taken from dishpans filled with water. As will be seen in a later chapter, the infant and child mortality rate is high, partly due to unsanitary conditions but also because the women have many tasks to carry out every day, even if they are not employed. Children, especially boys, are often left to themselves for long periods.

Girls are usually kept closer to mothers than are boys. At a fairly early age, girls are told that they are "of the house," and they must begin to help with the cleaning, cooking, child care, and washing. Boys are usually much older before work is expected of them.

Another task done very often is clothes washing and ironing. Dominicans seem to be very conscious of dress, and they prefer to wear freshly washed and ironed shirts and dresses. In the villages studied, washing is a difficult task always done by hand. It often involves carrying the clothes a half-mile or more to an irrigation ditch or a stream. The clothes are usually dried at home, hung on fences or trees. Those with water at home are saved the long trip, but laundry is still a time-consuming task. After the clothes are washed and dried, they are ironed.

As mentioned in the previous section, women also sometimes take care of poultry and animals, feeding them, gathering eggs, catching and slaughtering them for food, milking cows or goats, and performing similar tasks. If they are part of a farming family, they sometimes help in the fields when many hands are needed. They also make coffee and take food and drink to the men in the fields.

The daily tasks of the women of these villages, then, are arduous and time-consuming. When women take on employment, they are typically still expected to carry out these traditional tasks as usual. In the following section, data from the survey are given about the family division of labor in these household tasks.

COMPARING WORKERS AND NONWORKERS ON HOUSEHOLD WORK

The four major tasks--food preparation, cleaning of house and kitchen, clothing care, and child care--are listed in Table 9.2, and for each is given the distribution of responses to the question "Who in the family does the following activities? Mention the person who has the major responsibility for each activity, and others who are helpers."

In the community sample, the respondent was almost always the principal food preparer, with daughters often being involved as helpers. Other household members were rarely involved in food preparation. By comparison, only two-thirds of the worker respondents were principal food preparers, with both daughters and mothers often taking over that task. The workers were more likely than the community women to be helpers rather than principal cooks.

In terms of cleaning and laundry, there are no striking differences between workers and nonworkers in having the principal responsibility for these tasks. The woman of the house or the daughter was, in both samples, most likely to have these responsibilities. The latter task is not necessarily done daily, so that it would be easier for working women to maintain some responsibility for it than for the more constant tasks of food preparation and child care.

For child care, workers were significantly less likely than nonworkers to have the primary responsibility, being supplanted at times by daughters and in other cases by mothers. In the last two tasks (clothes care and child care), the worker families appear to have developed a greater amount of task sharing than the others, as the great majority

Table 9.2
Principal Task Performer and Helper, by Type of
Task and Sample (percentages)

Task/Performer	Community sample		Worker sample	
	Principal	Helper	Principal	Helper
FOOD PREPARATION				
Respondent	90.6	2.6	67.1	8.6
Husband	0.0	3.4	0.0	0.0
Daughter	5.1	37.6	11.4	25.7
Son	0.0	1.7	0.0	1.4
Mother	0.0	0.9	13.0	7.1
Male relative	0.0	0.0	0.0	0.0
Female relative	4.3	6.0	5.7	12.9
No one	0.0	47.0	2.8	42.9
CLEANING				
Respondent	65.0	3.4	62.9	8.6
Husband	0.0	0.0	0.0	0.0
Daughter	25.6	32.5	25.7	22.9
Son	0.0	0.0	0.0	0.0
Mother	0.9	0.0	2.9	7.1
Male relative	0.0	0.0	0.0	0.0
Female relative	6.8	8.5	7.1	17.1
No one	0.0	53.0	1.4	44.3
CLOTHES CARE				
Respondent	76.9	3.4	71.4	8.7
Husband	0.0	0.9	0.0	0.0
Daughter	13.7	25.6	15.7	26.1
Son	0.0	0.9	0.0	0.0
Mother	0.0	0.0	2.9	5.8
Male relative	0.9	0.0	0.0	0.0
Female relative	6.8	7.7	5.7	15.9
No one	1.7*	61.5	4.3	43.5
CHILD CARE[**]				
Respondent	75.5	3.1	40.0	1.8
Husband	0.0	1.1	1.8	1.8
Daughter	16.4	18.4	18.2	27.3
Son	0.0	3.1	1.8	0.0
Mother	3.1	1.1	25.5	12.7
Male relative	1.1	1.1	0.0	1.8
Female relative	4.1	4.1	10.9	20.0
No one	0.0	68.0	1.8	34.5

[*]Nonfamily, hired help.
[**]Families with children only.

of worker respondents named both a principal and a helper, while in the community sample these tasks were usually done by one person. In addition, the extended family seems to play a more important role for the worker households--the mothers of respondents were more involved, for example, in child care and food preparation. Also, other female relatives were often involved in these tasks. Although one would expect that, during the working season, these women would need help with their household tasks, it is interesting to note that even in the subsample of workers who were not working at the time of the interview (the summer interviews), these differences in task responsibility remained.

Of course, it should be also noted that almost all of the changes in the household division of labor involved the sharing of or taking responsibility for tasks by other females-- daughters, mothers, sisters, nieces, or aunts. Almost never did the household division of labor include males as either principals or helpers. Thus, as in many other societies, women move into some formerly "masculine" spheres of activity much more easily and quickly than men move into traditionally "feminine" activities.

We do, however, see in the data some evidence of greater role sharing and extended family cooperation among females, within the worker sample. This network of female kinship both allows more flexibility in roles for some women and provides support in times of need. This role sharing, especially involving the mothers of the respondents, can also be seen in the responses to the question "Who takes care of the children while you work?" Of 54 workers who required help with their children, 28 (51.9 percent) received this assistance from their mothers, 9 from daughters, 7 from sisters, and 4 from their husbands. For the majority, then, the mother plays a very crucial role, allowing the woman to work away from home when otherwise it would be very difficult.

SUMMARY

We have seen that the major agricultural tasks of women in these communities center on the care of animals and poultry, with very low participation in the fieldwork. Although not all families were involved in these tasks, when they were done, tasks such as plowing, sowing, harvesting, and selling products were usually done by husbands, sons, or hired male workers.

In terms of the household tasks of cleaning, cooking, caring for clothes, and child care, the women of the representative sample had greater responsibility for these tasks than did the workers, and they were less likely to have help. The workers seemed to have developed a greater degree of cooperation among the female members of the family, especially between mothers and daughters. The workers' mothers were more frequently involved as principals or helpers in child care and food preparation, compared with the community sample. The older daughters, likewise, were more often involved in the household tasks. And the percentage of families in which both a principal worker and a helper were named was greater for the worker sample, indicating a more cooperative organization of work than in the traditional household. These changes persisted even for the workers who were not currently working at the time of the interview.

Women from Guayacanal carry laundry the half-mile round trip to and from the irrigation canal. The canal is the source of water for drinking, cooking, laundry, and swimming, in addition to irrigation.

Young woman hanging out her laundry. Her house is typical of houses in this community, made of *palma* with a thatch roof.

Young woman cooks beans and rice in open-sided, thatch-roofed kitchen while neighborhood children play.

A young woman stands in front of her Los Jobillos home with her daughter. On the table are a few vegetables and shelled beans that she has grown and prepared for sale to passersby.

Nutrition, Health,
and Contraceptive Use

One of the purposes of this survey was to obtain information about aspects of health and nutrition among the women in the communities, comparing workers and nonworkers. This information will help us to see what the level of health and nutrition is among the population in general, and to see if any effects of women's employment can be detected.

DOMINICAN DIET AND NUTRITION

Weil (1973:79) states, "The average Dominican diet is deficient, both in quantitative and qualitative terms. In the mid-1960s, the average per capita daily food intake was about 2230 calories, below the 2654 calories estimated to be the average for 17 Latin American countries during the same period." Data from a 1983 study (MUDE 1985:148) show that average caloric consumption in the country as a whole has actually declined in more recent years. Weil (1973:79) also states that the Dominican diet was lower than average for Latin America in terms of protein, vitamin, and mineral intake.

The situation is worse, according to Weil, in rural areas and among low-income urban residents (about 80 percent of the population). In these settings, the diet consists mainly of rice, red beans, starchy root crops, and bananas. Weil writes that green vegetables are hardly ever eaten, and that poultry or beef, though desired, is a rarity. Chickens are seen everywhere in rural communities, but they are too valuable as producers of eggs to be eaten. Fish, although abundant, is not usually considered good food by Dominicans (1973:81). Goats are often kept for milk, but their meat is a luxury reserved for special occasions such as Christmas. When chicken or beef is eaten, it is usually cooked as part of a stew (*sancocho*), along with root vegetables, in order to make it stretch further. Rarely is beef eaten as a steak, and the poor never consume it in that form. In cooking, almost all parts of animals are used--beef tripe is cooked in stew (*mondongo*), and chicken feet are cooked along with the other parts. Very little is wasted.

Another common food is sausage (*salchicha*) or salami, made locally from residual pork products. These are common meal items, along with fried eggs and plantains. For those who can afford it, a typical evening meal consists of fried eggs, fried sausages, and perhaps fried cheese--all cooked in a great deal of oil.

In all social classes, rice and beans seem to be universally served, with other dishes added as resources increase. Among the poor, there is little variation from the rice and beans--except that the ratio of beans to rice goes down, creating a diet based mainly on rice, with a small amount of beans and "bean juice" to flavor it.

NUTRITION IN THE AZUA COMMUNITIES

As a very basic measure of nutrition, the women were read a list of food items and were asked to indicate how often the family eats each item (if ever). The frequency of eating each item was classified into the categories "daily," "a few times a week," "occasionally," and "never." (This question is adapted from Cebotarev 1979.) Table 10.1 gives a summary of the responses to this list of items by sample.

A quick glance at the table shows a great deal of similarity between the two samples in their dietary patterns. For example, the two foods consumed daily by almost everyone are rice and beans, followed by milk and plantains. These foods make up the bulk of the diet among poor people in the Dominican Republic. The daily consumption of rice and beans is somewhat higher among the worker sample, suggesting less variety in their diets than in the diets of the community sample families.

In addition to rice, beans, milk, and plantains, there were considerable percentages of families in both samples eating eggs and meats at least a few times a week (though not

Table 10.1
Food Consumption of Families in Samples, by
Frequency of Consumption (percent reporting
consumption)

Food item	Sample	(A)Daily	(B) a few times per week	(A+B)	Never
Rice	Comm.	81.2	13.7	94.9	1.7
	Work.	96.6	3.4	100.0	0.0
Beans	Comm.	71.8	16.2	88.0	2.6
	Work.	89.7	10.3	100.0	0.0
Milk	Comm.	67.5	12.8	80.3	5.1
	Work.	72.4	13.8	86.2	0.0
Plantains	Comm.	67.5	17.9	85.4	3.4
	Work.	65.5	31.0	96.5	0.0
Eggs	Comm.	21.4	45.3	66.7	12.9
	Work.	24.1	37.9	62.0	6.9
Meats	Comm.	17.9	45.3	63.2	6.9
	Work.	20.7	37.9	58.6	3.4
Tubers	Comm.	18.8	27.4	46.2	9.4
	Work.	10.3	27.6	37.9	10.3
Eggplant	Comm.	3.4	35.9	39.3	24.8
	Work.	0.0	31.0	31.0	17.2
Greens	Comm.	27.4	9.4	36.8	35.9
	Work.	20.7	17.2	37.9	34.4
Fruits	Comm.	12.8	22.2	35.0	23.9
	Work.	6.9	20.7	27.6	24.1
Salads	Comm.	0.0	25.6	25.6	22.0
	Work.	0.0	10.3	10.3	20.3
Corn	Comm.	9.4	8.5	17.9	24.0
	Work.	0.0	10.3	10.3	31.0
Fish	Comm.	2.6	16.2	18.8	15.4
	Work.	0.0	24.1	24.1	37.9
Cheese	Comm.	0.9	20.5	21.4	40.2
	Work.	0.0	24.1	24.1	37.9
Oatmeal	Comm.	1.7	5.1	6.8	50.4
	Work.	3.4	6.9	10.3	51.7

usually daily). These, of course, are also good sources of protein, and there are not any noticeable differences between workers and nonworkers on those items.

Items consumed at least a few times a week by at least 25 percent of one or both groups were fruits, salads, eggplant, greens, and tubers (potatoes, yucca, yams). For most of these, there seems to be a greater tendency for women in the community sample to report using the items. This would again suggest somewhat less variety in the workers' diets, especially with regard to vitamin- and bulk-providing foods such as fruits and vegetables. For these items, however, it should also be noted that a significant percentage of both groups said they "never" ate them. Those foods eaten only occasionally were fish, corn, oatmeal, and cheese. A number of women mentioned spaghetti as a frequent meal item. In all, it appears that the majority of families get their protein primarily from the combination of rice and beans, which, if eaten together and in sufficient quantity, fulfill the body's protein needs. However, in discussing the typical rural diet with a local nutritionist, it was pointed out to me that the balance of the rice-bean combination is often too heavily weighted toward the cheaper rice, with insufficient beans to provide the necessary protein balance. It seems likely that this is also the case for these families. Milk also provides a complete protein, and is consumed daily by about two-thirds of the families. However, it is likely that most of those who consume milk are children, as most older Dominicans do not drink much milk. Meat and eggs are eaten at least a few times a week by about two-thirds.

Thus, depending on the calorie consumption and balance of items, it is possible that basic protein needs are met, but deficiencies may exist in vitamin- and bulk-providing foods such as fruits and vegetables. There also seems to be little variety in the diet, and the worker group appears to be a bit worse off in this respect.

The women were asked how many meals they usually eat per day; the modal response was "two" for both samples. There were no important differences between the two samples on this, with over a fourth reporting one or one or two, about 42 percent of each sample reporting two or two or three, and about 28-30 percent reporting three meals as the usual practice.

This was followed by the question "When there is not enough food for the family, who eats more and who eats less?" This question was an attempt to tap subtle forms of discrimination against females, as it has been reported in some studies that it is usually the females who eat less if someone must.

The most common responses for "who eats less" in the community sample were "adults," "children," and "all eat equally." The respondent and/or "females" were about three times as likely to eat less as were the husband and/or "males." In comparing the responses with those of the worker group, it was apparent that the workers were more likely to eat less in times of scarcity, and that children were less likely to be called on to sacrifice their food portions than in the community sample. The most common category of persons in the worker sample reportedly eating less was "adults," with "all equally" also being quite common.

From these data, we see the pattern that females appear to be more likely to sacrifice nutrition than males in times of scarcity, and that (perhaps) the workers are more likely to be protective of children's eating rights. However, more study is needed before any conclusive interpretations can be made from these observations, due to the small sample sizes and the variability of answers.

HEALTH AND CHILD MORTALITY

The women were asked a few questions dealing with health or health knowledge. The first was "How many times in the past year did you go to the clinic (you or another person in your family)?" For the community sample, the range was from "none" to 30 times, with a median of 2 times; 35 percent reported no visits to the clinic within the past year. For the worker group, the range was from "none" to 25 times, also with a median of 2. For this group, 27.6 percent reported no visits to the clinic during the past year. Overall, there do not appear to be any notable differences between the two samples in the number of visits to the clinic reported for the past year, but a relatively large percentage of both groups reported no visits. A number of respondents commented that although there was a "clinic" located in their community, it was not equipped and had no personnel. Thus, in order to see a doctor, they had to go into Azua.

The women were also asked if there had been any illnesses in the family, either in adults or in children, within the past month. About 38 percent of the worker women and 27 percent of the nonworker women reported at least one adult illness. In addition, 31 percent of the workers and 27 percent of the nonworkers reported having at least one child who was ill during the month. The groups were about equally likely to have consulted a doctor about these illnesses: 26 percent and 28 percent of the community and worker samples, respectively. And 74 percent of the community group and 78 percent of the workers had consulted a doctor about children's illnesses. So both groups were much more likely to see a doctor about a child's illness than about an adult's.

The women were also asked where their last baby had been born and who assisted at the birth. For the community sample, some 15 percent had had their last baby at home, with the other 85 percent having been at a clinic or hospital. For the worker group, the figures are similar: 17 percent of last births had been at home, and 83 percent in a clinic.

In response to the question of "who assisted," 54 percent of the community sample but only 44 percent of the workers had a physician present at the birth of the last child. About a third of the community women had a midwife, and a few had either a nurse or someone else (mother, friend, or, in one case, husband). The workers were slightly more likely to have had a midwife, a friend, or a relative in attendance. Thus, even though the great majority of these births took place in a clinic, many did not have a physician in attendance. The quality of midwife care, like the quality of physician care, probably is highly variable.

The majority of women in both samples usually breast-fed their babies, the most common period for both samples being 12 months (the nursing period for about 40 percent of each sample). However, the worker group was somewhat more likely to have stopped breast-feeding at an earlier point, with 44 percent nursing for less than a year, compared with 35 percent of the community sample. Similarly, about 25 percent of the nonworkers had breast-fed for more than a year--10 percent for two years. By comparison, only 15 percent of the workers had breast-fed for more than a year. Part of this difference is due to age differences; older women nursed their babies for longer periods. The difference is also due to the difficulty of working outside the home if a baby is still nursing. Among working women we would expect to see earlier weaning of babies, and that expectation is borne out by these women's experiences.

The women were asked at what age they began to supplement the baby's diet with foods other than milk. In the United States, the current consensus of most doctors seems to be that anywhere between three and five months is a good age to begin this practice. In general, six months and later would usually be considered later than ideal, and less than three months, too early. For both groups, the modal age was three months, accounting for 37 percent of the working mothers and 27.6 percent of the community sample. The largest group of women within each sample was in the recommended range of three to five months. The main difference is that the worker group was more likely to begin other foods before the age of three months, and less likely to wait until six months or later. Some 39 percent of the women in the community sample had not given additional foods until after the baby was six months old, compared with 26 percent of the worker sample. When they did add foods to the diet, the most common foods given to the baby were milk, eggs, and potatoes, with soup, "fruits," and beans (or the "soup" of beans) mentioned quite often. A few mentioned various cereals (cream of wheat, oatmeal, cream of rice, or the water in which rice was cooked) and noodles. About a fourth mentioned "meats" and a few mentioned fruit juices--especially lemon or orange juice. Only very rarely did they mention prepared baby foods, and no one mentioned any green or yellow vegetables.

The women were also asked if their children had been "vaccinated." Due to the successful recent vaccination campaigns of the national government, the percentage responding positively was high: 89.6 percent of the community sample and 96.2 percent of the worker sample.

Finally, questions were asked about child mortality. Some 49 women in the community sample (41.9 percent) had had at least one child die, as had 18 (25.7 percent) of the worker sample. The members of the community sample were more likely to have experienced the death of more than one child, with 21 percent of the women in that category, compared with 17 percent of the workers. The Dominican Republic as a whole has a high child mortality rate, compared with other Latin American countries, and these figures are a stark reminder of that fact.

The above figures represent all deaths of sons or daughters of the respondents, regardless of age, including a few deaths of children who were adults at the time of their deaths. For example, 6 of the 87 deaths reported in the community sample had occurred after the child had reached his/her eighteenth birthday. The child mortality rate, counting only deaths of children under age five, as a proportion of all reported live births, was 71 deaths out of 742 births, or 96 deaths per 1,000 births.

By comparison, the worker sample had experienced 22 deaths of children and 272 births, for an overall death rate of 81 per 1,000 births. All but one of these had died before the end of the eighth year, and almost all before age four. Fourteen of the 22 deaths had occurred in the first year of life. The child mortality rate for workers was lower than that for the community sample, 62.5 deaths of children aged up to 4 years per 1,000 live births. Thus, the workers had relatively fewer children die, and a smaller percentage of the women had lost children. The community sample, which included more older women, had more often experienced the deaths of older children and a few adult children, but they had also had more young children die.

An interesting demographic characteristic of the Dominican Republic is its sex-specific death rates by age. In most countries, the male death rate at any particular age is greater than the female rate. There are relatively few countries in the world in which the female mortality rates are greater than the male. This phenomenon usually occurs in areas of strong male dominance and female subordination (such as the Muslim countries of the Middle East and parts of India). It is also the case for the Dominican Republic, unlike most other Latin American countries. We find evidence for this even in the small sample of children's deaths we have been discussing. In the worker sample, of 22 deaths for which this information was given, 8 were of males. Similarly, for the community sample, of 65 deaths for which detailed information was gathered, 29 were of males and 36 were of females. In all, then, there were 37 male deaths and 50 female deaths, or 1.35 times as many female deaths. Clearly, caution is necessary here, because of the small sample size and the variability of this ratio, but these figures do go along with other statistics on mortality by gender in the Dominican Republic. Unfortunately, lower value of the female in a society can result in such behaviors as subtle neglect and less vigilant care, leading ultimately to higher death rates for females (Retherford 1975; Weeks 1986:158).

Causes of death of the children who died were also detailed for up to two children in each household. Table 10.2 gives the list of these causes for the two samples. As in most Third World settings, the leading cause of death among children was diarrhea and/or dehydration, accounting for 21 percent of the deaths of children in the community sample. This was followed by accidents of various kinds, including burning, drowning, a fall, and unspecified accidents. The next leading cause of death for children was reported to be *mal de*

Table 10.2
Causes of Death for Children who Died,
by Sample

Causes	Community sample		Worker sample	
	n	percent	n	percent
Diarrhea/ dehydration	14	20.6	2	10.5
Mal de ojo/ las brujas	6	8.8	3	15.8
Premature	5	7.4	4	21.1
Accident	8	11.8	1	5.3
Born ill	3	4.4	1	5.3
Died in child- birth	3	4.4	0	0.0
"Colerin"	2	2.9	1	5.3
Tetanus	2	2.9	0	0.0
Pneumonia/ bronchitis	2	2.9	3	15.8
Diphtheria	2	2.9	0	0.0
Whooping cough	1	1.5		
Meningitis	1	1.5	0	0.0
Chicken pox	1	1.5	0	0.0
War of 1965	1	1.5	0	0.0
"Bad milk"	0	0.0	1	5.3
Typhus	0			5.3
Diabetes	0			5.3
Unknown/unable to classify	17	20.6	3	10.5
Totals	68		19	

ojo or, in one case, *las brujas*. *Mal de ojo* is usually translated "evileye," and *las brujas* means "the witches." Thus, for a significant proportion of children who die (probably due to indiscernible causes), the people blame witchcraft or an "evil spell" or a "curse" placed on the child by someone with evil intentions.

In addition, a number of children died after being born ill or premature. Several children (a significant proportion) died of infectious diseases for which vaccines or cures are available--for example, tetanus, diphtheria, whooping cough, and pneumonia. One could probably assume that many of these deaths could have been prevented with modern vaccines and/or antibiotics. Since there were only 19 causes of child deaths given for the worker sample, those are not analyzed in detail, but the causes of death listed for that group do not appear to differ significantly from those of the community group.

CONTRACEPTION AND FERTILITY PLANS

The use of contraception is often an important determinant of women's participation in productive economic activities, as well as their general status in society. As long as women are burdened with pregnancies and child rearing throughout their reproductive years, they usually cannot hope to accomplish much in the spheres of activity outside the boundaries of the home. Furthermore, birth limitation can improve not only the woman's well-being but the health and standard of living of her children as well, as each child can receive more attention, care, and resources for education, nutrition, and other needs.

However, in situations of high infant mortality, as well as in rural agricultural economies, fertility control has not found great acceptance, nor has it been effectively utilized by women. Where child mortality is high, more births are often desired to ensure that at least some children will survive to adulthood. In rural subsistence farming, children are often seen as assets to the family, extra sources of unpaid family labor who will contribute more to the family's economic base than their cost (see Lappé and Collins 1978:30-33). In addition, in Latin America, there is some resistance to contraceptive use for religious reasons, because of Roman Catholic opposition. There is also a strong psychological connection between "masculinity" and paternity. Finally, in a culture where male dominance is strong but communication between spouses is weak, contraception is not likely to be widely used (Lappé and Collins 1978:30-39). Thus, there are many reasons to expect that the typical woman of the communities studied is not a user of contraception.

On the other hand, since the women who work for wages for the large companies are somewhat more independent from male dominance, since they depend on wages and not family farm labor for survival, and since they seem to prefer marriage in which there is more communication between spouses, it is reasonable to expect that they might be more favorable toward the use of contraception than their traditional sisters. One other motivating force is the greater difficulty of combining pregnancy, lactation, and infant care with wage labor outside the home. In other words, if these women want to continue working, perhaps they see the benefit of avoiding pregnancies or at least of spacing them.

As shown in Table 10.3, the majority of women in both samples said they had not thought about using contraception, although, as expected, the worker group did include a higher percentage who had thought about it. Similarly, the workers had a higher actual use rate, according to the responses to the question "Have you ever used any contraceptive method?" Thus, while 41 percent of the workers had thought about contraception, compared with 30 percent of the community sample, about 38 percent of the workers and 27 percent of the nonworkers had actually used some method.

Only a few women reported that they currently used contraception--about 5-7 percent. In addition, about 12 percent of the community sample and 21 percent of the workers said they had been surgically sterilized. So, adding these to the percentage still using contraception (they did not interpret sterilization as a "contraceptive method"), we find about 28 percent of the workers and 17 percent of the community sample actively avoiding pregnancy through contraceptive practice.

Those who had never used any method were asked to explain why not. The reasons were scattered and often vague, but one of the most common reasons given by the nonworker respondents was that contraception is "harmful" or "dangerous." Out of 61 responses to this question, 14 (23 percent) gave this as their reason for not using contraception. Other reasons were "these things weren't used in my day," "I never needed it," or "I wanted (want) my children." No one mentioned objections from husbands or the fear of being left without children when growing old. There seems to be a strong pronatalist bias among these women, and an anticontraceptive bias as part of that. It is also interesting to note that no one mentioned religious reasons for opposing contraception. Thus, reasons often given by researchers for lack of contraception use by women such as these were not the reasons given by the women themselves.

The nonusers among the worker sample gave similar responses, although they were much less likely to express fear of the "harmful" nature of contraception. The most common response was "I don't like it." The most common contraceptive method that had been used was the contraceptive pill, reported by 53 percent of the community sample ever-users and 73 percent of the worker sample ever-users. However, as mentioned before, almost all of these

Table 10.3
Contraceptive Use in the Two Samples
(percentages)

Contraceptive use	Community sample	Worker sample
Have "thought about using"	30.2	41.4
Have actually used	26.5	37.9
Still use	5.1	6.9
Surgically sterilized	11.9	20.7

women had stopped using contraception by the time of the interview.

Those women who had at one time used a method and who no longer used it were asked why they had stopped. There were very few responses to this question, but the most common (7 out of 12) was "it harmed me" or "it made me feel bad." One woman had been warned by her doctor that it was dangerous. Thus, there is apparently a fear of contraception that is stronger than the fear of the sterilization operation and prevents women from using it effectively. This fear may be reinforced by local physicians. On the other hand, it is possible that the types of contraceptive pills usually given to poor women do have negative side effects, which then cause the negative attitude toward their use.

SUMMARY

In this chapter, we have seen that the basic diets of the women in these samples were somewhat monotonous, consisting primarily of daily rations of rice and beans, with plantains, eggs, and meat or poultry usually eaten a few times a week. The community sample appears to be somewhat better off, in that they reported having a more varied diet, perhaps due to their greater involvement in farming and animal raising.

The workers were less likely to say that the children ate less when there was not enough to go around. For both groups, women were more likely than men to eat less in this situation. There were no important differences in the number of illnesses in the families of workers and nonworkers, and both were much more likely to consult a physician for a child's illness than for an adult's illness.

The majority of both groups had given birth to their last baby in a clinic or hospital, not at home, and about half had been attended by a physician, the remainder mainly by a nurse or a midwife. Most women breast-fed their babies, but the workers stopped nursing at an earlier point, although for both groups the most common period of breast-feeding was one year. The workers were somewhat more likely to have begun giving other foods to the baby at earlier ages.

The women in the community sample were more likely to have lost a child through death, even when only young children were considered. The sex-specific data on deaths among children show that a higher percentage of those who died were female, and the female-to-male death ratio was higher than would be expected under "normal" conditions. The leading causes of death were diarrhea, accidents, and *mal de ojo*.

The use of contraception was very low, although the workers were more likely to have tried some form of contraceptive. The workers had a higher percentage of surgical sterilizations, the most commonly reported method of birth control.

On some measures, the workers seem to have slightly poorer health records, which probably results from their origins in poorer economic circumstances. They do, however, appear to have more positive attitudes and practices with respect to contraceptive use, and their children are slightly better off with respect to child mortality. Thus, while the results are mixed, there is some evidence that employment is associated with improved conditions for children and lower fertility, both important for the future of these women and their children.

11 Childbearing, Education of Children, Hopes for the Future

In this chapter, we look at the actual childbearing of the women in the samples, compared with their ideal family sizes, and various aspects of their attitudes toward the rearing of children. Any differences in the aspirations and expectations that these women have for their sons and for their daughters, or between workers and others, will be of interest. Are the workers' aspirations for their sons and daughters, for example, less traditional than those of the women in the community sample?

The lack of effective use of contraception described in the previous chapter inevitably leads to greater fertility than is desired by the women in these communities. This is demonstrated in the responses to the two questions "How many children have you had?" and "How many children do you think is the ideal number for a family?" The community sample members reported having had an average of 6.3 children, more than the 4.3 average for the workers (Table 11.1). For many women, these were not "completed" family sizes, so that the average number of children these women will eventually have is undoubtedly higher than the figures given. Even so, the average *ideal* number for both samples was smaller, especially for the women in the community sample. Their ideal number of children averaged 3.9 (2.4 fewer than their actual average), compared with an ideal family size of 3.2 children for the workers (0.8 fewer than their actual family size at present). Although the difference between ideal and real family size was smaller for the workers, they also had a slightly larger percentage who

Table 11.1
Number of Children Born to Respondents, by
Sample (percentages and cumulative percentages)

N. children	Community sample		Worker sample	
	%	Cum.%	%	Cum.%
None	1.8	1.8	4.4	4.4
1	0.9	2.7	11.8	16.2
2	6.3	9.0	13.2	29.4
3	13.5	22.5	20.6	50.0
4	3.6	26.1	13.2	63.2
5	10.8	36.9	11.8	75.0
6	15.3	52.2	8.8	83.8
7	9.9	62.1	5.9	89.7
8	7.2	69.3	5.9	95.6
9	9.0	78.3	0.0	95.6
10	11.7	90.0	2.9	98.5
11	2.7	92.7	0.0	98.5
12	4.5	97.2	0.0	98.5
13	1.8	99.0	0.0	98.5
14	0.0	99.0	1.5	100.0

18	0.9	99.0	0.0	100.0
	(n=111)		(n=68)	
	Mean = 6.3		Mean = 4.0	

expected to have more children (24 percent versus 15 percent), so that this difference might narrow before all of these women complete their childbearing.

A much higher percentage of the community sample women had large families--for example, 46.8 percent had seven or more children, compared with only 16.2 percent of the workers. This may be explained partly by the greater contraceptive practice of the workers, the greater percentage of divorced/separated workers, and the greater motivation to have fewer children in order to work. The younger age of the workers is probably another factor in explaining their lower fertility and fertility ideals.

The women were asked if they were currently pregnant. Those responding "yes" were 10.3 percent of the community sample and 7.1 percent of the workers. The fact that the workers contained a greater percentage in the childbearing ages would lead one to expect a higher pregnancy rate among them, other things being equal. The lack of difference is another bit of evidence of lower fertility among the workers.

The greater fertility of the nonworker group means that they have more children actually living with them in the household, which means a greater support burden for each household. Over 40 percent of the community sample households contained five or more children, compared with only 24 percent of the worker households. On the other hand, over half of the worker households had two or fewer children, compared with only 31 percent of the community sample.

GODPARENTS

Godparenting is usually considered to be an important social institution in Latin America, and it has been described as such by scholars writing about the Dominican Republic (see Weil 1973 and Cross-Beras 1980, for example). Godparents are said to play important roles in the socialization and support of children, acting as "coparents." In a poor community, godparents can provide important support when parents' resources are strained. However, the degree to which godparents actually function in this way varies, and one question of interest in the present study was the extent to which the tradition of godparenting was carried out by the families in rural Azua. The women were asked if their children had godparents, and what the godparents did. Over 90 percent of the women said their children had godparents, but when asked what the godparents did for the children, their responses indicated that the role of godparents was very limited. About half of each sample said that the godparents did "nothing." The next most common response was "they baptize them" or "give them the blessing" at the christening, but nothing else. Only in a minority of cases did godparents play an active role in the lives of the children: In about 10 percent of the community sample families, the godparents gave the children gifts for *los Reyes*, the traditional day of gift giving (January 6) associated with the Christmas season. In addition, about 7 percent of each sample said that the godparents "visit" the children and/or "love" them. Perhaps these are the most active in their role as godparents. Finally, a small percentage of the women said that godparents help when a child dies, buying the casket or in other ways aiding the bereaved family. On the whole, the traditional institution of godparenting does not seem to function significantly for these people except at the baptism of the child.

ASPIRATIONS FOR SONS AND DAUGHTERS

Respondents were asked a number of questions about their hopes for their sons and daughters, including the age at which they should marry, educational goals, and occupational aspirations for daughters. The purpose of these items was, first, to see how sex-role attitudes affect these aspirations, perhaps resulting in different goals for daughters and sons. Second, it was to see if these goals differ for the workers and for the community sample women. We might expect that the workers would have higher educational goals for their children, for example, because they themselves have broken some of the traditional norms concerning occupational roles.

Educational Aspirations

Educational goals for children were assessed by the responses to the question "What do you want for your daughters (sons); for example, how many years of education do you want them to complete?" In general, the educational aspirations of these women for their children were much higher than their own mostly primary-level educational attainments. Only 15 percent of the community women and 19 percent of the workers wanted their daughters to complete less than 12 years of schooling. Almost 60 percent of the community sample wanted their daughters to go beyond high school (12 years), and about 23 percent wanted them to go beyond 16 years. The corresponding figures for the worker group were 68 percent and 32 percent, respectively. Thus, the worker group had slightly higher aspirations than the others. It is not clear if these women understand exactly what "16 years" of education refers to, but they are very positive about the goal of education for their daughters.

When comparing educational aspirations for sons with those for daughters, we find that in both samples a slightly higher percentage wanted sons to go beyond high school. In the community sample, 65.9 percent wanted sons to go beyond 12 years (compared with 57 percent for daughters); the comparable figures in the worker sample were 75.8 percent for sons and 68.2 percent for daughters. The worker sample, then, appears to have higher aspirations for their sons than for their daughters, and for both sons and daughters, higher aspirations than do the women in the community sample. The median levels of education desired for sons were 15 years for the community sample and 16 years for the worker sample.

Marriage Age

The women were also asked at what age they hoped their daughters and sons would marry. Educational attainment, especially for women, is usually directly related to age at marriage. The most common age specified as desirable for a daughter's marriage was 20 years. The community sample women were more likely to mention younger ages (33.3 percent gave an age under 19, compared with 14.3 percent of the workers). About 30 percent of each group gave ages greater than 20, with 25 being a fairly common response. Medians for both groups were 20 years. Thus, the age at which marriage is desired for daughters is, on the average, about three years later than the average age at which these women married. Interestingly, that age is about the age when one would expect them to have completed the median educational level desired, 15 years, assuming continuity in school attendance. The only notable difference between the samples is the greater tendency of workers to hope that their daughters will wait until they are at least 20 before they marry.

For sons, marriage age aspirations were quite different. The majority of both samples hoped their sons would marry at age 25 or later, with the mode and the median being 25 years. The two samples were similar, in that 54 percent of the community sample and 59 percent of the workers gave 25 years or older as the ideal marriage age for sons. Only 10 percent of each group gave ages under 19. No real differences were noted between workers and nonworkers in their aspirations for their sons' marriage ages.

Occupations

The women were asked what type of occupation they would like their daughters to have. The responses to this fell into three groups: traditional feminine occupations such as housewife or seamstress; highly female-dominated but modern occupations such as nurse, secretary, or teacher; and modern professional occupations, such as agronomist, engineer, physician, or lawyer. There were few noticeable differences between the two samples. Almost all respondents hoped their daughters would have an occupation outside the home. Only 6 percent of the community sample, and none of the workers, gave a traditional female occupation as a hoped-for goal for their daughters. Around 25 percent of each sample mentioned a highly female-dominated modern occupation, and about 40 percent mentioned a profession. One is struck by the high aspirations that all of these women have for their daughters, and by the absence of the mention of traditional roles. In fact, only four women of the entire 216 said they hoped their daughters would be *amas de casa* (housewives). In this sense, then, the women of these rural communities are very different from women in earlier generations, or at least we can assume so.

MOST IMPORTANT THINGS TO TEACH SONS/ DAUGHTERS

Finally, respondents were asked, "What are the most important things to teach to daughters/sons?" The responses to these questions were diverse, but by far the most common response for both sons and daughters was "education" or "to study"; 83 percent of the community sample women and 69 percent of the workers gave education as one of the important things to give a daughter. Similarly, 77 percent of the community sample and 76 percent of the workers mentioned education as one of the most important things to teach a son. For daughters, the next most common response type was that she should learn to cook, to clean, and so forth-- that is, to do the traditional household chores (*los oficios de la casa*). Next came good manners and behavior. No other response was very frequent as something to teach daughters. The strong emphasis on education, even greater than the traditional women's activities, is important.

For sons, after the major goal of education came the traditional male activity, work. For about half of the community sample and almost half of the workers, one of the most important things to teach a son was "to work," or "to have a profession," or (for example) "to be a good farmer." So, although the women put education above other things for both sons and daughters, they followed that with household chores for daughters and work skills for sons. Again, other responses were not very frequent. A few women mentioned such things as "to be responsible," "to be serious," or not to steal or drink too much. These last two items were never mentioned for daughters. However, overall, the responses show a strong belief in education as a goal for both daughters and sons, and there is not much difference between the two samples on this.

EDUCATIONAL PROGRESS OF CHILDREN

As a measure of current educational progress of the children of these women, the years of school completed by age of child were computed, as follows. Assuming that children begin school at age six, then by age seven they should have completed roughly one year of school, at age eight, two years, and so on. This assumption is more valid for those interviews done in July, after the school year was complete, but most respondents gave current year of school for "years completed" in the March interviews as well. We can get a rough idea of how well the children in the household are keeping up with their educational level by seeing how far ahead or behind their grade-for-age level they are. This was done by subtracting the grade the child *should* have completed if he or she attended as expected for his/her age group from the actual grade completed. For example, if a seven-year-old had no education, then the educational deficit would be one year. If an eight-year-old had zero years of school, that would be a deficit of two years. If a ten-year-old had completed one year of school, then that child would have a three-year deficit, since a ten-year-old should have completed four years. Of course this is not a precise measure for individual cases, but as a rough estimate for group comparisons of means it is adequate to give us an idea of the relative advantages or disadvantages of the groups.

This index of educational advantage was computed for all 427 children between ages 6 and 18, inclusive, in the households sampled. Male children in the community sample had a mean educational deficit of 3.2 years, compared with 3.0 years for females. The children of worker households were slightly better off, with mean deficits of 2.4 years for males and 2.4 years for females. Thus, on average, the workers' children had about half a year's advantage over the community children. However, both sets of children were behind, and it seems unlikely that their mothers' aspirations for them will be fulfilled.

SUMMARY

The community sample had an average of two more children per woman than the workers, and will probably still have more children after both groups complete their childbearing. Both groups have significantly more children than they say are ideal for a family, although the gap between the ideal and the real is greater for the community sample. Although the great majority of children have godparents, for three-fourths or more the only thing godparents do is to participate in the baptismal ceremony. Only in a small minority of cases were godparents involved with their godchildren even at the level of gift giving for *los Reyes*.

Educational aspirations for sons and daughters were high, with aspirations for sons being higher for both groups. Workers were less likely than nonworkers to think that their daughters should marry at very early ages. For sons, marriage-age aspirations were much higher, with little difference between the samples.

The responses on the most important thing to teach sons and daughters show the strong value that these women place on education for both sons and daughters, with higher expectations for sons. Finally, the occupational aspirations mentioned for daughters by the women in both samples showed hopes for occupations that were nontraditional and, in around two-fifths of the cases, professional in nature.

In summary, both groups have high aspirations for their children, but the workers tend to have higher aspirations in terms of education (for both sons and daughters) and marriage ages (for daughters). In addition, the workers have fewer children, which means that they will perhaps have more resources per child to help them reach their educational and occupational goals. This is supported by the data on actual educational progress of the children, which show greater deficits in educational status among the children of the nonworking women.

In March 1986, a follow up set of more qualitative interviews was carried out with 41 women workers who were employed at that time. A number of questions were asked about their attitudes toward their work and its problems. The majority expressed positive attitudes toward their work, saying that their working caused no problems for them within their families. However, when the married and unmarried workers were compared, the married women were likely to express more problems as a result of working--mainly problems with their husbands' attitudes.

Of 29 married (in-union) women surveyed, 12 (41.4 percent) said that their husbands opposed their working. Several of these women said that the husband's opposition had led to increased arguments and fighting, but they did not consider quitting work as a solution to those problems. Among the responses were the following:

> He doesn't like it, but I have to work; I do it for
> my   children.

> He doesn't like my working, but I have to. He
> doesn't   like it because he has to take care of
> the children while I work.

> He doesn't like my working, but I have to
> because of the high cost of living.

> My husband doesn't like it, but I don't care. It
> doesn't really create problems.

The majority (17 of the 29) of in-union workers said
that their husbands either supported their working or at least
did not interfere.

The problems spoken of by the working women tended
to center on the difficulty of carrying out their traditional
housework and child care functions while working:

> The main problem is that I can't clean the
> house and take care of my children when I'm
> working.

> I really can't attend to my husband and my
> house as I should.

A few women mentioned serious problems with the
husband as a result of his opposition, including separations
and increased fighting. A typical response was the following:

> He opposes my working; he gets angry and
> fights. He's become an enemy, refusing to
> speak to me or even to look at me.

For the single-mother worker, conflicts related to
working were less common. Most of the problems mentioned
had to do with the difficulty of caring for young children and
taking care of housework. Said one woman:

> The children have to be left alone, with no one
> to feed them. They go hungry, with no one but
> God to watch them.

Three others of the 12 single-mother workers in this group
mentioned attending to children as the major problem
created by their work. The majority, however, said that their
work caused no problems for them or their families.

These women were all asked, "What aspects of your
work would you like to change, if you could?" The most
common response was "nothing" or "everything is fine" (12 out
of 41). Among the others, the work schedule was the most
frequently mentioned aspect that the women would like to
change. They begin in the morning around 10 o'clock, and
they work through the day until 6, 7, or 8 at night. This gives

them little time to do the work at home that they must also do, and is an exhausting routine.

These women also frequently complained about the type of work they do. Many would prefer to do less physically demanding work. For example, they would prefer something "more comfortable," such as office work or work in a business, or even a change from, say, working with corn to working with melons.

A few women also said they would prefer to work closer to home, or to have transportation provided. And six women said they would like better pay, because the work they do is very hard. Overall, the aspects of work that the women would like to change are understandable, given the types of work done. The most serious difficulty seems to be the long workday, which makes it impossible for many of the women to do necessary work at home, given both time constraints and fatigue. As we saw in Chapter 9, many of these women have resolved some of this problem through reliance on female kin to help with household work and child care. Overall, however, the attitude of most of the workers is that the work is good--they would rather be working than not. Only 2 women of the 41 interviewed said they would prefer to quit working altogether, but they could not afford to.

In summary, the women who work for the large agricultural companies in the Azua region seem to be satisfied with their work, because it provides them with much-needed income. For a few, husbands' opposition to their work caused difficulties at home, but these women had chosen to continue working because of the important economic benefits. In addition, the problems of child care and housework were frequently mentioned as important difficulties of working, but these problems were often resolved by cooperation of the extended family. The most commonly mentioned aspect of work that these women would like to change was the schedule, which runs morning to evening.

13   Individual Portraits of the Women of Rural Azua

In this chapter, eight women are singled out for detailed description. Four are workers; four are not. They vary in age, marital status, and life history. The purpose of these descriptions is to put a human face on the analysis given in this book, to present a picture of some of the variety one can find within the community, and to illustrate in greater detail some of the associations and characteristics discussed in the previous chapters.

CRITELA: 32, MARRIED, TOMATO PACKER FOR DOMEX

Critela was interviewed in Pueblo Viejo in March 1987. She is 32 years old, married to Rafael, age 45; they live with their 6 children. The oldest, Neido, is a 16-year-old boy, followed by Escania, 12; Clifar, 11; Eskin, 7; Nander, 6; and Martina, 4. Critela cannot read, having completed only one year of school. Her husband completed three years of school, and so is "literate." Following in their parents' footsteps, the 16-year-old boy has completed third grade; the 12-year-old daughter and 11 year-old son, second grade; and the younger children, none.

The family lives in a concrete block house with a cement floor, electricity, and running water. They have a refrigerator but no radio, television, or electric fan. They own the house, as well as 18 *tareas* of land (about 3 acres), which they cultivate. Their main crops are tomatoes and corn, for their own consumption and for sale.

Most of the farm work is done by Rafael and Neido. Neido helps with planting, plowing, and harvest; Rafael alone applies chemicals and sells the produce.

The family has small animals, which are cared for by Nubia, Critela's sister, who comes in to help with the housework while she works for DoMex. Nubia is responsible for cleaning the house and kitchen, washing and ironing clothes, and care of the young children. She is helped with the cleaning and child care by Escania, the older daughter. Critela is primarily responsible for food preparation, with help from her sister.

Critela works as a tomato packer for DoMex, where she earns RD$450 per month, a higher-than-average salary for the women in this sample. She has worked there for three years, for six months each year. At the time of the interview, she was still working. Her earnings are the family's primary income source. She says that her husband doesn't give her enough to support the family because the harvest is too small.

"He doesn't like it that I work," she says of her husband. She worries that she can't attend to her husband or her house properly because of the job. In addition, the hours are too long. Nevertheless, she chooses to work.

In spite of these problems, Critela was able to pay for the family's food, clothing, educational, and housing expenses during recent months. Her husband paid only for house repairs. Her income seems to be going directly for family needs, and represents the main source of support.

Perhaps because of her important contribution to the family, Critela has considerable control over family decisions. She says she both decides and controls spending money for food, clothing and shoes, education, medicines, housewares, and housing. In addition, she claims to make decisions about the children's education, and she keeps the family's money.

Critela was born in Pueblo Viejo and has spent her entire life there. She grew up primarily with her mother, in a very large family of 12 brothers and 8 sisters. She left home to join her *marido* at age 15. Critela had her first child at age 16. She has had eight children, two of whom have died. Both of these died in the first year of life, one daughter at nine months and a son at six months. The daughter died because of *brujas* (witchcraft) and the son of a "fever."

When asked how many children she thought were ideal for a family, she said, "Four, because things are so hard today; before, things were less expensive." Like most women in this study, Critela had more children than she thought ideal. She has been sterilized and therefore expects no more children. She never used contraceptives before her operation.

When asked what are the most important things a mother can teach her children, Critela responded in very traditional ways. Daughters should be taught "to clean the house, to cook and iron," while sons should be taught "to study and to work." She would like to see both her daughters and her sons complete high school, a goal not likely to be reached, given her children's present educational level. She gave 20 as a good age for both sons and daughters to marry. For both, she thought that "teacher" would be a good occupation. She hopes to see her daughters marry the kind of man who "earns a paycheck" and who gives them what they need for the family.

Critela says she is generally satisfied with her relationship with Rafael. She believes the free union to be better for a person in her situation, because "one is tied down" (*amarrada*) if she marries legally. Her notion of a good husband is one who takes care of his wife "like a father." But many men are not good husbands because they drink too much. The typical *maridos* in the community, she says, are "both good and bad, but some go so far as to hit their women."

Critela is Catholic and she knows the priest, though she never goes to see him. She attends the local church about once a year, and her husband never goes. However, like many in Pueblo Viejo, she prays daily even though she is not much involved with formal religion. Her children have godparents who "baptized" them but otherwise are not involved.

She rests "on Sundays," which is also when she enjoys herself. Her favorite form of entertainment is dancing, and she and Rafael dance on Sundays. He also drinks rum on those occasions, but Critela does not. The person she feels closest to is her mother.

Overall, Critela seems to be relatively satisfied with her life. She likes her work and has money to contribute to the family. She has a better-than-average house, and the family seems to eat better than many, with a varied diet and three meals daily. She has a fairly important role in decision making at home, and she works even though her husband doesn't like it. Her life reveals certain advantages that accrue to those who move into the world of employment, but she also benefits from the fact that the family has a small *parcela* to work.

DAMARIS: 32, MARRIED, COOK FOR A.B.C.

Damaris, a 32-year-old Pueblo Viejo resident, lives with her *marido* Benjamin and their four children. The children are 13, 8, 7, and preschool age (the exact age of the youngest was not given). The family lives in a wood-and-*palma* house with cement floor but no electricity or running water. The house is lighted by a kerosene lamp.

Damaris was born in Pueblo Viejo, but she has lived in three other places, including La Romana, in the eastern part of the country. She says she has 15 brothers and 13 sisters, almost surely the result of multiple unions of her parents (half siblings and stepsiblings are usually referred to as brothers and sisters). Although both parents are living, she spent most of her childhood with her mother's parents. Her mother now lives in San Cristobal, about 40 miles to the east, near Santo Domingo, and her father lives in Pueblo Viejo. She sees her mother only once or twice a year.

At age 12, Damaris left home to go into domestic work taking care of a child. At 17, she married, although that relationship did not last long. A son she had in that union now lives with his father. The oldest son in the household is also from the first union.

Damaris's *marido* is Benjamin, age 47. He completed eighth grade, while she went no further than the second. Benjamin works for the government (in Azua) as a policeman, earning RD$250 per month. Damaris works for A.B.C. as a cook, earning RD$150 per month, six months per year. Benjamin has been a policeman for 16 years. Damaris has worked for A.B.C. for two years. While she works, a cousin (male) takes care of the children. If there were really young children (0-3 years), this arrangement would probably not be the same, since men almost never take care of infants and young children. Her work, Damaris says, has not caused problems at home, because her husband "favors it and doesn't say anything."

Out of the RD$250 a month earned by Benjamin, he gives RD$80 to Damaris for the household. From this, and with her own money, Damaris pays for household expenses. She says she controls expenditures for food, clothing, and shoes, but her *marido* controls the money for education, medicine, and household furnishings. Most of her own money goes for food and clothing. Although she "keeps the family's money" and "decides how to spend it," a large portion of Benjamin's earnings are defined as "his," and thus are not given to her. Decisions about the education of the children are made jointly. The overall power balance seems to lean toward the husband, although Damaris's earnings give her more control than she would have otherwise.

All household work is done by Damaris, without any help--this includes food preparation, laundry and ironing, cleaning of the house, and care of the children. The family has no poultry, animals, or land in cultivation, so there are no agricultural tasks to perform.

Although the family does not have electricity or plumbing, they are not as poor as some. Nutritionally, they may be better fed than many, for although they eat only two meals daily, they do consume milk, eggs, beans, rice, plantains, and vegetables daily, according to Damaris. A few times a week they eat meat and salads, and occasionally they eat cheese, fish, fruits, and other cereals. Compared with many family diet reports, this one seemed relatively balanced and varied.

Damaris's last baby was born in a hospital, the birth attended by a physician. When one of her children was ill with a fever during the past month, she took him to the doctor for medicine.

It is possible that the diet and medical practices of Damaris's family are due to increased concern brought about by the death of three children. Damaris has had eight children in all, and only five are alive today. One two-year-old son died of a fever, and two were stillborn (or died soon after birth). (Dominican women count stillborn and even miscarried fetuses as children, so that the number of children reported by a mother is sometimes higher than in our own accounting system.) Her *ideal* number of children is two, "because one used to be able to have many children, but today you can only take care of a few." Again, the difference between ideal and actual family size is great. Still, Damaris uses no contraception, even though she doesn't want to have more children. She prefers neither boys nor girls, because "both help their mothers."

Damaris' *union libre* of 11 years is about what she expected, although she is not especially happy with it. She believes it would be better to marry legally, "because there's more respect in marriage." A good husband, she says, is one who understands his wife. In her community, the typical man is good to his wife. Wives should understand their husbands and "not find fault with them."

When asked about her aspirations for her daughters, Damaris hoped they would get 15 years of education, be married at age 20 to "a man who has studied," become doctors, and "live well." For a son, she hopes he will get 20 years of education, marry at 25, be an engineer, and "marry a woman who will respect his mother." For all her children, she wishes that they live well "in their own house."

Damaris is a Catholic, baptized as an infant, but she claims no religion now, although her children were baptized and have godparents who "help them with money." She does not know the local priest; neither she nor her husband attends mass or other religious services; and she never prays. She rests in the afternoons, and enjoys "drinking and dancing" on Saturdays and Sundays. Her husband enjoys drinking rum "every day." She makes a trip into town (Azua) about once a month. The person she feels closest to is a neighbor woman. Damaris definitely seems less traditional in attitude and behavior than many women, perhaps because she has lived in several places, she is married to a policeman, and she has supported herself since age 12. The one thing she would change about her job is the money: "If I could earn 1,000 pesos, I could build a house--they pay me very little."

ARGENTINA: 27, SEPARATED, FIELDWORKER FOR BARCELO

Argentina lives in Ansonia in a zinc-covered house with electricity, running water, and concrete floor, with her four children, ages 8, 6, 4, and 11 months. She is separated from her *marido*, whom she married at age 15. She is now 27.

Argentina was born and has lived her entire life in Ansonia. She grew up there with both parents, six brothers, and five sisters. Her parents still live in the community, and she sees them every day. Her mother is the one she mentions as the person she feels closest to. She attended the local school for four years, so she knows how to read.

The children are left in the care of a neighbor woman when Argentina goes to her job at Barcelo. She is a fieldworker, weeding tomatoes for RD$240 a month. At the time of the interview, she had been working for a month, and this was her first year with the company.

In addition to her earned income, Argentina receives some help from two younger sisters, one in Venezuela and the other in Puerto Rico. Both migrated in order to find work, and both work as private household domestics. They send money and clothing to the family in Ansonia. Argentina has no other financial support; she receives nothing from her children's father.

She does have help with the household chores from a neighbor. The neighbor cooks and looks after the children, with some help from Argentina's eight-year-old daughter, Feni. Argentina takes care of cleaning the house and doing the laundry. Feni also helps with the clothes. The family has no animals or poultry to take care of.

The diet of this family is typical of the poorer families-- daily rations of beans and rice, with milk for the baby. A few times a week the family eats meat, eggs, or fish, and plantains or yams. Vegetables, salads, and fruits are hardly ever eaten. Unlike most women in the study, Argentina nursed the last baby for only one month.

Argentina married at 15, and had her first baby at 17. She remained with her *marido* for eight years, and has been separated for four years. She believes that legal marriage would be preferable to *union libre*, because in marriage the couple is "more united." Many local men, she says, are "bad at home," not taking care of their wives or helping them.

Daughters should be taught to clean the house and have a "good education," and sons, "to study and to work." She would like to see her daughters complete 16 years of school, marry "a professional" at 20, and be doctors. She has the same occupational and educational hopes for her sons, but she wants them to marry at age 25 and have wives "who are their equals." She hopes that "they grow up to be someone."

Argentina is Catholic and attends mass two or three times per month. Her children have godparents, but they receive "nothing" from them. Her life seems very limited-- she says she rests on Sundays, but when asked what she does for enjoyment, her response was "nothing." Similarly, to "when do you enjoy yourself?" she responded "Never."

She prefers daughters to sons, because "they're better, they love and help their mother more than boys." When asked how many children she thought were the ideal number for one in her situation, Argentina answered "three, because then you wouldn't have to struggle so much."

AURELIA: 76, MARRIED, NONEMPLOYED

At 76, Aurelia is one of the oldest women in the study. She lives in her *palma*-walled house in Ansonia with her *marido*, Bienvenido, who is 82. A grandson, age 11, lives with them. Aurelia completed one year of school, but she is unable to read and write. Her husband had no formal education, and he also is illiterate. The grandson, Nander, has finished first grade and can read and write minimally.

Aurelia was born in San Juan de la Maguana, a city some 30 miles to the northwest of Azua. Unlike the great majority of Ansonia residents, she grew up in an urban setting. Also unusual, she spent her childhood years with her godmother instead of her natural parents. At age 15, she left home to marry her present *marido*, with whom she has been for 60 years. They have spent the past 30 years in Ansonia.

The couple own their house, which has both electricity and running water. They also own about one acre of land, but they are too old to work it. Their income is from Bienvenido's job as a school caretaker, which brings in RD$250 per month. Although Aurelia says that she decides how to spend money on a list of specific expenditures (food, clothing, repairs, and housing), she said her husband controls each one.

Aurelia still does the household work, including food preparation, cleaning, and clothing care, as well as care of poultry and animals. She receives help with the latter task from a son, but she does everything else alone.

This couple has had 18 children, perhaps typical of their generation. Three of these children died as infants. She never used any form of contraception, because "they didn't do that in those days." Aurelia's first child was born when she was 13 years old, before she left home to join Bienvenido. When asked how many children she thought ideal for a family now, she said none, because things are going from bad to worse.

Aurelia's idea of a good husband is one who not only treats his wife well but also is "loving" (*amoroso*). She believes that not many men are like this, because "there aren't many like mine." In this community, the majority of men are "corrupt." She believes that formal marriage is better than the *union libre,* "because one lives very united, with much love."

When asked about goals for daughters and sons, Aurelia was fairly traditional. Daughters should learn domestic duties and to study, while sons should be taught a trade, such as carpentry. Daughters should have 10 years of school, and marry at age 15. They should be "of the house" and not have a modern occupation. She says she hopes her daughters will be very happy, and that their husbands " will be good, like my husband."

For sons, she thinks the best marriage age is 18, and hopes that they have as much education as they want and that they find good wives. Her ideal marriage age for both sons and daughters is, then, lower than that of most younger women.

Aurelia is Catholic, and more active than most women studied. She knows the priest, visits him monthly, and attends mass with her husband every week. She also prays every day.

She and her husband enjoy sitting together and talking as their main diversion. She never goes to Azua, but she does participate in a women's organization in Ansonia.

Their children are now grown and gone from home. Julio left home at age 25 to go to Santo Domingo, where he is a policeman. A daughter, Florida, left at age 10 (she is now 33). She also is in the capital, working as a seamstress. Another son works at a shop in Santo Domingo. Five others are in other places, mostly married; the other daughters are not employed. These distant children visit occasionally and help with finances.

Perhaps it is her age, but Aurelia seems to have a better relationship with her husband than most women studied. One wonders if this is a generational difference, an aging effect, or a personal trait. Whatever the reason, of all respondents, she spoke more positively of her husband and their relationship than most, and she was one of the few who mentioned "love" as an aspect of her own marriage and a desirable trait in a husband. The contrast with the cynicism about men of younger women was striking.

PERCIA: 29, MARRIED, NONWORKER

Percia, age 29, lives with her husband Luis (age 30) and two children in Las Barias. They own their cement-floored, wooden house, which has both electricity and running water. She was born in Azua and has spent most of her life there. Both of her parents still live in Las Barias, and she sees them every day.

Percia and Luis own five *tareas* of land (less than one acre), on which they grow tomatoes and corn. This is the only source of income for the family. Luis does all of the fieldwork on this land, although he pays others to help with the sowing. The family has no animals or poultry. Percia does the cooking, cleaning, laundry, and most of the child care, with some help with the latter task from her eight-year-old daughter, Trinidad. She does not participate in the agricultural fieldwork.

Percia completed fourth grade, and Luis completed fifth, so both can read. The eight-year old has completed two years of school, and the six-year-old, one year.

Percia left her parents' house to join Luis when she was 19. The first child was born when she was 20. They have had three children, one of whom died at age three months. This infant died while she was away from the house looking for firewood--no one was home with the child at the time.

Decisions in this household are made primarily by Luis. He decides how to spend money on almost all specific expenditures mentioned, including food, clothing, housing repairs, and implements. Percia says that she decides about money for education and household needs, but that Luis "controls" the money for all of these expenditures. In addition, she says that Luis makes the decisions about the children's education, and he keeps the family's money. Furthermore, unlike most others, even her vote in the last national election was decided "by my husband."

Percia seems fairly content in her marriage. She says her union with Luis has been better than she expected. She believes the *union libre* to be better than legal marriage, because "in the country people don't know how to carry out marriage. So it's better to be free than married."

Her idea of a good husband is one who "does whatever I tell him I need, and doesn't make me go without." Most husbands, she thinks, "are men who drink a lot." A good wife, on the other hand, is one who doesn't "do wrong" to her husband, and for whom "whatever she has is for them both. If I have 100 pesos, it's for him." One gets the impression here of a marriage that involves a great deal of sharing and understanding.

Percia thinks that three children is an ideal number for a family, "because things are so bad, and with more than three, you don't have the means to educate them." She does expect to have more children, and in fact was pregnant at the time of the interview. She prefers boys to girls, because "boys work and can help me."

Percia is pregnant in spite of an attempt at contraception. Her method, however, was to drink a special tea recommended for the purpose, and "I wound up pregnant using it." The use of such home-remedy contraceptives is fairly common among rural Dominicans; more effective methods are distrusted.

Daughters and sons should be given a good education by their mothers. For sons, however, "the first thing is to not steal and to not hurt anyone." The prevention of such negative behaviors in sons is often mentioned by the women in this study.

Percia hopes to see her daughters finish 18 years of schooling, to marry "professionals" at age 25, and to be nurses. She hopes her sons will get 19 years of education, marry at 28, and marry "good women." She says she would like her sons to grow up to be ballplayers or doctors.

Percia is Catholic. Her children were baptized and have godparents. The godparents recognize the children by giving them gifts for *los Reyes* (January 6, the day the Wise Men were supposed to have visited the baby Jesus in Bethlehem, and the traditional gift-giving day in the Dominican Republic, rather than December 25). She knows the community priest, but she does not attend mass. She does pray daily, however.

Both Percia and Luis enjoy dancing, and occasionally they go to a bar for that purpose. She also goes to Azua once a month. When asked who was the person she felt closest to, she responded, "my husband, Luis."

Overall, Percia seems to be a rather traditional young woman for whom the traditional roles are working, probably because the family has a small plot of land that is its own. Even though her role in the household is relatively powerless, she is included in her husband's entertainment activities, and the two seem to have a close relationship. Perhaps the traditional roles work best where traditional resources are also available--a home owned and land worked by the family itself.

MINERVA: 25, MARRIED, NONWORKER

In Guayacanal, perhaps the poorest village of the several studied, Minerva was interviewed in her wooden house. The house has electricity, water, and a cement floor, and the family owns it. Minerva is 25 and lives with her free union husband, Victor, who is 40, their three children (ages 7, 5, and 2), and two step children, both age 12. She has lived in Guayacanal all of her life, having grown up there with both parents and 15 siblings. Her parents still live there, and she sees them daily. She has been living with Victor since she was 17.

Minerva never attended school, and so she is unable to read or write. Victor completed fifth grade, as did his 12-year-old son. The daughter finished third grade; the little ones have not yet begun school.

The family has no land and no cattle. Minerva is unable to report any income-producing activity. When asked what the major source of income was for the family, she answered, "There isn't any." Although the family must have (or must have had) some income, it clearly is very little. In stating expenditures, she reported only 100 pesos a month for food, and none for education, medicines, house repairs, or household goods. Clearly this family is very poor.

Minerva says that she and Victor both make decisions about spending money, but he is the one who "controls" the money. He also decides about the children's education, and he keeps the family's money. She says, "I have to stay beneath my husband, because he's the boss" (*el es que manda*).

In the list of household tasks given in the survey, Minerva reports doing all of them without help, including cleaning, cooking, laundry, child care, and care of poultry.

The family usually eats only one or two meals a day. The nutritional data given were among the worst in the sample. Only milk and rice were reported as being eaten daily, and the milk was for the children. Beans were reportedly eaten "a few times a week." All other items (meat, eggs, fruits, plantains, potatoes, and so on) were eaten only "occasionally." All of these have to be purchased, except for eggs and fruit, which are given to them or otherwise obtained without cost. No one in the family went to a clinic during the past year, which probably results from their poverty, not their health.

Minerva has had three children, all of whom are still alive. The first was born when she was 18. She thinks that three or four is an ideal number for a family, "because it's very hard to have many children." She does not want to have more, although she is now pregnant with a fourth child. She took contraceptive pills for a while but stopped "because one has to be well-fed to use these pills."

Minerva's marriage to Victor, she says, is "worse" than she expected, although she does not elaborate. She believes that the *union libre* is preferable to marriage, "because this way, if one wants to marry, she can, but if they don't get along well, she can leave." A good husband, she says, is one who is "peaceful in the house."

Minerva is very traditional in her sex-role expectations. She says she does not go out, so she cannot say what the typical men of the community are like. She wants to teach her daughters "their duties" in the household, as well as educate them. Her sons should learn "to study and to work."

She hopes her daughters will complete 8 years of school and marry at 18 to "a good man who won't disgust them." She had no specific occupational hopes for her daughters. For her sons, she hopes they will get 12 years of education, marry at 20, marry a "good and pretty woman," and "work at their profession."

Minerva is Catholic, and so are her children. Although they have godparents, they do "nothing" for them. Neither Minerva nor Victor attends church, and she also says she does not pray. Her husband goes out every day, but she stays home. Only "every three months" does she go into Azua. Still, she says her husband is the one person she feels closest to.

This woman is very poor, and she demonstrates some of the limitations of the traditional life when resources are too few. She depends on her husband for support, but he cannot give it. She is not happy, but she has few options for change. She wants no more children, yet she is pregnant. She seems almost totally isolated in her home with her children and household duties. She does see her parents and probably her siblings, but she seems tired and older than her 27 years.

BEATRIZ: 24, MARRIED, MELON WASHER

Beatriz lives in Ansonia with her 24-year-old husband, her 60-year-old widowed mother, her 106-year-old grandmother, five nephews and nieces ranging in age from 19 to 6, and her own 2-year-old son. They live in the family's house of wood and *palma*, which has a cement floor, electricity, and running water. The house has a radio, television, and electric fan, but no refrigerator.

Beatriz grew up in Ansonia with both parents and 12 brothers and sisters. Her father is now dead. The family owns 30 *tareas* of land, all of which is cultivated. They raise tomatoes, cantaloupes, and corn for their own consumption and for sale. Work on the farm is done by Eddy, Beatriz's husband, with occasional help with plowing from his brother.

Beatriz finished seventh grade, and Eddy finished eighth. Neither her mother nor her grandmother attended school at all. Beatriz and Eddy are relatively well educated for Ansonia residents.

Beatriz works as a melon washer in one of the melon-exporting companies, where she earns RD$200 a month. She began working this year, and will work for three months. Her mother keeps the baby while Beatriz works. She says that her work brings in more money than the *parcela*, "because the harvest is so poor it hardly makes anything." In addition to these sources of income, a sister and her family in Venezuela send money to help.

In this household, most decisions are made by Beatriz and her mother. It is clear that the house and land belong to Beatriz's family, and that Eddy has moved in with his wife. This is not the usual pattern, and the disadvantage for Eddy is that he has little power within the household. On all household expenses either Beatriz or her mother decides and controls the expenditures. When the family needed a loan in the past year, it was Beatriz and her mother who obtained it. Beatriz also keeps the family's money and decides about education for the nieces and nephews.

Household duties are carried out by female members of the family: Food preparation, clothing care, and cleaning are done mainly by Anania, the 19-year-old niece. Delia, the mother, cares for the children and the poultry. Eddy does all the farm work.

This family has three meals a day, and their diet seems better than average. Every day they have a variety of foods, including milk, fruits, cheese, beans, rice, plantains, and *verduras* (greens). Often they also have eggs, meat, salads, oatmeal, yams or *yucca*, and spaghetti. The family seems to be doing relatively well.

Beatriz married Eddy at age 20. They have had one child, born two years later. She is happy with her marriage, saying it is better than expected. She believes that the *union libre* is better than marriage, because of the legal trouble of divorce: "If one wants to leave and she's married, she has to get involved in a lot of paper."

Beatriz thinks five is an ideal number of children, because one can educate them better than if she had more. She expects to have more, but she is likely to have more control over how many and when than is typical in these communities, for she is currently taking birth control pills. This sets her apart from many others, although it is not uncommon for her age group and educational level.

Daughters should be "taught the things of the house and given a good education," and sons also should "be educated." She would like to see her daughters get 16 years of education and marry at 25. She would also like to see them become doctors and marry "a man who is both good and faithful, and who doesn't mistreat them." For her sons, Beatriz hopes even more: that they complete 20 years of education and marry at

30, that they be engineers, and marry "a woman who will make them happy."

Beatriz is an active Catholic, attending mass every week, although she does not pray on her own. Her husband does not attend church. Beatriz goes into town every week to go shopping. She says she rests in the evening, and enjoys dancing on Saturdays and Sundays with Eddy. On those days, he drinks rum.

Beatriz's working has not caused problems at home. Eddy "supports me, he's not opposed to my working." The only thing about work that she would change is the schedule. "I go at ten in the morning, and don't get home until six, seven, and eight at night. If I could change anything, that would be it."

Beatriz represents a younger, better-educated woman in these communities. Her attitude is less tied to tradition than average. One gets the sense of a woman who means to control the choices in her life, not just accept traditional expectations. Her position in her mother's family, her education, and the resources available to the family probably give her this ability to forge her own way with a degree of independence not common among rural Dominican women.

VALERIANA: 53, WIDOWED, *FREIDORA*

Valeriana, 53, lives with four sons, one daughter, and a 17-year-old nephew. She was born in Fondo Negro, a rural community near Azua, and grew up there with her mother and five siblings. Her mother is no longer living. She has lived in Fondo Negro, Cotui, and Los Jobillos, having spent the last 32 years in the latter.

She gives her marital status as "widow." She has had two marriages (unions), the first at age 13. She left her first husband after a year, "because he lived in Cotui and I didn't want to be there." Her children are mostly grown now, those at home ranging in age from 14 to 29.

The educational level of this family is somewhat higher than average. Valeriana has completed fifth grade; the older sons have completed the sixth, seventh, and eight grades, respectively; and the 14-year-old daughter, fifth grade. One son did not attend school and does not read.

The family owns its house and a small plot of land--three-fourths of a *tarea*--on which they grow bananas for their own consumption. They have no cattle, other animals, or poultry. Their main source of support is from Valeriana's work as a *freidora*, a vendor of fried foods. At this job, she makes about RD$50 a month, working ten hours a week. In addition, she receives some help from relatives living outside the country.

Since she has no husband and has her own income, Valeriana is the main decision maker in this household. The sons and nephews sometimes work as agricultural laborers for others, contributing some money to the household.

Household work is done by Valeriana and her daughter Ondina, with the daughter having full responsibility for cleaning and clothes care. Valeriana is the main food preparer, with help from Ondina.

Valeriana has had ten children, nine of whom are still living. One son drowned in an irrigation canal when he was 14. Her first child was born when she was 14, in her first union. She believes that four children are an ideal number for a family, "because the situation isn't very good for having so many children." She never used contraceptive methods, "because before, the people were ignorant, and also I don't like them."

A mother should teach her daughters "the household duties," and her sons "to work," Valeriana says. She hopes her daughters will study "as long as they are able," and marry at 18. She does not want them to have to be employed, but to be *amas de casa* (housewives). She also hopes they will marry "good men, even if they're poor," and have a good destiny. For her sons, she simply hopes they will marry whenever they want, to intelligent women, and also have a good life.

Valeriana says she does not think there is much difference between legal marriage and the *union libre*, "because rather than have a bad time with a companion, it's better to have a bad time alone. . . . The men of today are *malos* [bad]."

Valeriana was baptized Catholic, as were her children, but she never attends mass, nor does she pray. Like many in the study, organized religion is not important in her life. On the other hand, the festivities associated with funeral wakes are seen as times of diversion for Valeriana. She especially enjoys dancing *los palos*, which is associated with these festivities, with African rhythms provided by drums, sticks, and singing.

Valeriana lives in a bamboo house with an earthen floor. The house has no electricity or plumbing. She goes to Azua once a week, to sell her fried goods. Otherwise, she stays close to home. She feels closest to her youngest daughter, Ondina, with whom she shares most of the household duties.

As we come to the end of this book, we should stop and review the basic findings about the women in the rural communities we have studied. In general, we have found that although the women are poorly educated and lack economic resources, their hopes for their children are much higher. Life in the region is difficult, however, and it is not clear that the sons and daughters of these women will grow up to meet the expectations of their mothers, since they are already behind in their educational progress.

One new trend in the area (as in most parts of the world) is the increasing economic activity of women. Of course this can be exaggerated, since we saw that in reality only a very small percentage (12 percent) of women in these communities work for wages. Thus the impact of the companies is not great in the sense of changing the roles of many women in the community. In our study, we have seen that the women workers are younger than average, although women of various age groups, both married and single, were among those employed.

An important purpose of this study was to compare workers and nonworkers in order to see if any effects of paid employment could be detected. It seemed reasonable to expect, for example, that workers, due to their income, might have improved levels of living, health, and nutrition. Because they are "nontraditional" in their work role, they are perhaps less traditional in their approach to family planning and contraceptive use. And because of greater access to economic resources, it was expected that the working women would have more control over decision making and the use of resources within the home. Finally, it was expected that changes in the household division of labor might occur as a result of women's work outside the home. On most of these issues, our expectations were borne out.

The earning of income by women is a potentially important agent of change with families in the Dominican Republic, more so than increased earnings by men alone. In discussious about this problem with others who are familiar with development programs in the Dominican Republic, it has often been asserted that when rural men begin to increase their earnings, they are likely to increase their spending on their personal activities and not on the family. The woman's "allowance" for food, clothing, and household needs may remain constant, while the man's spending on the traditional male activities of drinking, gambling, and establishing relationships with other women increases. The extent to which this actually occurs is debatable, and has not been adequately documented, but it is generally recognized as valid by those who are familiar with rural Dominicans.

In our survey, we did find a strong tendency for men to engage in these activities fairly frequently. In response to the question "What does your husband do for fun?" the majority of women surveyed mentioned such activities as drinking, dancing, and gambling (about 70 percent of each sample). When asked how often he does these things, the responses tended to cluster in the "daily" to "weekly" range. In addition, some of the men were said to have other women or other families that took a portion of their income.

At any rate, given the woman's traditional responsibility for the care of the family and children, it is reasonable to assume that her earnings would be more likely than the man's to be spent on such things as food, clothing, house repairs, and education, with a lesser portion spent on personal diversion. (For women, the most commonly reported types of entertainment or diversion were visiting friends or family, watching television or listening to the radio, and "doing nothing," activities that do not cost money.) Thus, remunerated jobs for women might be expected to result in more benefits for children and for families than similar jobs for men.

In reality, evidence of improved levels of living among workers is not very striking in our study. However, when we remember that the workers more commonly came from the "poorest of the poor"--those with no land resources, no help from relatives, and a high percentage of single-parent families--their situation seems better than others with similar backgrounds. Having started at a relatively low economic position, we might have expected them to have lower ratings than average on housing, nutrition, and so forth. The fact that there were only small differences, some of which favored the workers, still supports the general claim that these women are significantly better off because of their work. At any rate, for the great majority of the workers, their earnings (and for some, the earnings of their husbands) were the main source of income for the family. Without their earnings, their families would have undoubtedly been significantly worse off. In the qualitative interviews with workers, the majority gave as their primary reason for working the economic benefit, frequently saying that they worked because they had to, in order to survive and to feed their children.

In terms of marital and family differences found between the two samples, the workers were more negative in their assessments of men and of marriage, and had less stable marital histories. The fact of employment is probably both cause and effect of the greater marital instability, as discussed in Chapter 7. It is a cause, in that the traditional role of women in the family is strained when they take on full-time outside employment. Husbands who might be happy with the extra income of the wife's earnings may resist the necessary changes in household affairs that result from employment. A number of women reported that their husbands did not like their working and that friction between the spouses had increased as a result. Also, once the women have their own income, they may feel more able to leave an unsatisfactory relationship, since they are not so dependent on the husband as in the traditional marriage. The workers were mostly happy to be earning the income provided by their jobs, in spite of husbands' complaints.

The very fact of being separated or divorced (or having an "unstable" marital history) is also a great motivating force for women's finding employment. Thus employment is also an effect of marital instability, so that the observed association between the two phenomena cannot be interpreted to mean that working causes family breakdown. There is no doubt, however, that employment gives women a degree of independence that they did not have before. This can have important effects on family dynamics.

We saw that the division of labor within the home seems to have undergone important changes within workers' families. The workers themselves were less likely to assume full responsibility for all domestic work than were the community sample women. They had a significantly greater degree of cooperative help from the female members of their families, including the extended family. They were more likely to share responsibility for the various tasks, and their mothers, sisters, aunts, and cousins were often involved in this helping network. Changes were only rarely noted in male activities or responsibilities within the household in response to women's work. But the female extended kinship network made possible the work activities of many women, providing a way to work and keep the household running at the same time. Those workers who had no help of this type were most often bothered by their inability to care properly for their children.

The workers also had more power and control over resources within the family. This evidence seems clear on a variety of measures. Compared with the women in the representative sample of community members, the workers made more decisions and controlled the spending of money to a greater extent. Because of this, and because of the women's traditional role as those who care for children and family welfare, we can assume that the families and children are better off.

As evidence of this, the children of workers were less often asked to "eat less" in times of scarcity. Workers were also more likely to limit their fertility, which means that they probably are able to provide better for the children they do have. The infant death rate was lower as a result. The workers also had higher aspirations for their children, an important psychological factor in the eventual accomplishments of the children. This was true for both occupational and educational hopes. There was a fairly strong rejection of the traditional woman's role of housekeeper, since the great majority of women in both groups hoped to see their daughters become paid professionals. Overall, in the sense of status within the household and control over their own lives, the workers seem to be better off than their more traditional counterparts. Their use of contraception, their employment, their aspirations, and their independence show a tendency to actively confront the future, making decisions and taking actions to promote their own interests. These women were not the "passive" women of common stereotypes. The findings of this study thus show clear evidence of some improvements in the lives of these women associated with their employment.

Finally, the workers are happy to be earning m
though they have a number of complaints about the wor
do. For some, husbands' resistance to their working
problem, but they usually do not consider this to be a
obstacle. For a minority, serious marital problems had arisen
due to the husbands' objections, but the women chose to work
to help their children, even if it meant losing their husbands.
Many women also had little help with the household work,
which caused difficulties. The most serious problem of this
sort was the lack of child care for those who did not have
female kin or friends who were able to take on this burden.
The other problems mentioned had to do with the working
conditions--especially the physical strain and the long hours
required.

In going back to our original question about the impact
on the women of employment at these companies, several
conclusions can be drawn. First, in the short run, the workers
are better off than they would have been without
employment, because of the immediate effect of having an
income. This income, on a fairly predictable basis and (for
many) over a several-year period, means that the women can
begin to take more control of their lives and their families'
lives. They have more control over decisions within the
family, and greater ability to end an unsatisfactory
relationship with a husband due to increased independence.
Perhaps as a result, they become more active and confident in
their plans for the future: considering contraception, rejecting
large families, hoping for better things for their children.
And in an immediate sense, they are able to make purchases
for themselves and their families that would have been
impossible before.

All of these positive effects, however, are the effects of
simply having an income, which provides a resource for
gaining control and independence within the family. Thus,
the income helps to break down patriarchal relations within
the individual family. Saying this does not imply, however,
that the type of employment that generates this income is
positive in its overall impacts on the women.

As in other contexts, the women are paid less than men,
and less than a "decent living wage," precisely because they
are discriminated against in the larger patriarchal economy.
They have no options for better wages or working conditions
because of this discrimination. Thus, they can obtain the
work only because they are marginalized in the general
economy.

The work done by these women is difficult, the hours are long, and the season is short--from three to six months per year. There are no new skills learned that could be used to move into better positions. And there is no protection against unfair labor practice, unsafe conditions, firing due to pregnancy, or similar problems. The conditions are not likely to change, and the future for these women and their children is, at best, repetition of the present.

An additional problem in this situation is the fact that the foreign-owned companies do not have any commitment to the area or the workers. During the year I was there, one company closed unexpectedly and moved to a new site in Venezuela, leaving former employees jobless once again. There were stories in the newspapers about damage done to the soil by the overuse and misuse of chemicals, which, according to the reports, had reduced the harvest and left the soil sterile in many formerly fertile areas (*El Sol*, 1987:1, 3). Furthermore, there is no guarantee that the companies will stay, so the hopes generated by the women's employment may be illusory, as has been true in so many similar cases (Lim 1983).

Thus, the long-term impacts of multinational industrial developments of the type studied here are not really positive at the local level. They do not impart transferable skills to the labor force, nor do they integrate the workers (especially the women workers) into the larger industrial labor force. The work is highly stressful and without benefits or advancement, or even assurance of a future. All of these factors contribute to the continuing marginality of women as workers, not to their long-term improved status. While temporary improvements in self-image, economic independence, and feelings of solidarity with other workers may result, giving rise to the noted changes in marital power and family roles, the overall impact is clouded by the lack of security and impossibility of advancement. Thus, we have learned, again, that women do well when given opportunities to be independent and to earn income, but that most of the opportunities given them are extremely restricted by the overall patriarchal nature of society at large. Development in which women maintain control over the means of their subsistence would therefore seem to be more promising than increased dependence on economic organizations whose loyalties and interests lie elsewhere. This means placing more resources in the hands of women, training in useful skills, promoting self-sufficient cooperative endeavors, and providing support such as adequate schooling and child care.

Although these goals may seem unrealistic within the present geopolitical situation, they seem appropriate as goals to work for if genuine progress for women and their children is to be made.

Appendix A   Interviewer Instructions

ENTRENAMIENTO PARA ENCUESTADORAS

A. INTRODUCCION

El propósito de esta encuesta es investigar las condiciones de vida de las familias y, particularmente, de las mujeres de esta zona. Nos interesa indagar lo que piensan sobre su situación actual y cuales son sus aspiraciones y expectativas para el futuro.

El cuestionario es necesariamente largo debido a que se ha debido cubrir una amplia gama de tópicos con el fin de obtener una descripción lo mas comprensiva posible de la vida comunitaria. Ésto incluye descubrir cualquier problema de salud o económico y constatar su posible causa y, en general, describir el modo de vida de la gente.

B. METODO PARA LAS ENTREVISTAS

1. Nosotros le indicaremos la vivienda y la persona que usted debe entrevistar. Procedera entonces a localizar dicha vivienda y a la persona (especificamente la jefa de la casa) y realizar la entrevista. No podra sustituir esta persona por ningún otro miembro de la familia sin la previa autorización nuestra.

2. Si en la vivienda no hay mujeres, proceda con la próxima entrevista en su agenda.

3. Si usted no puede concluir la entrevista por completo en un mismo día, haga lo mas que pueda y concerte una cita para el día siguiente (de ser posible), o lo mas pronto que pueda, para terminarla.

4. Si la persona encuestada le pregunta, "¿Por qué usted me hace esa pregunta?" o "¿Por qué usted quiere saber eso?" contéstele que estamos tratando de estudiar las condiciones de vida de las mujeres de esta comunidad, y que toda esa información es muy importante para nosotros. También nos interesa saber sus opiniones, pero al mismo tiempo se les hara saber que la información obtenida es estrictamente confidencial y anónima.

4.1. Es posible que algunos de los resultados de este estudio tengan un impacto positivo a nivel de los proyectos del gobierno y otras instituciones o agencias nacionales y extranjeras.

4.2. Parte de la información sera utilizada en la preparación de un libro acerca de la República Dominicana, y por tanto, es muy importante que sepamos lo que realmente piensan y cuales son sus aspiraciones.

5. Las entrevistas deberan conducirse sin la presencia de otros adultos. Especialmente no deben haber HOMBRES, dada la naturaleza de la mayoría de las preguntas.

6. Mantenga su neutralidad con respecto a las respuestas que obtenga de las encuestadas. No muestre ni verbalice sus opiniones personales. Si usted no esta de acuerdo con una respuesta, no lo exteriorice aunque sea con gestos de la cara. Trate la respuesta como cualquier otra: Trate de mostrar interés en todo lo que digan, siempre y cuando sean honestas en sus respuestas. Si usted manifiesta opiniones o juicios positivos o negativos, éso podría influenciar las demas respuestas que obtenga luego. Por tanto es recomendable actuar de una manera cortés, pero seria y con un poco de formalidad.

7. Antes de entrar en materia, preséntese a la encuestada.

7.1. Explíquele que usted estara entrevistando varias mujeres de la comunidad y que ella ha sido seleccionada para ser incluida en el estudio.

7.2 Explíquele que se trata de un estudio sociológico de las mujeres de esta zona, patrocinado por una universidad americana.

7.3 Si una persona esta indecisa o escéptica en cuanto a la entrevista, con cortesía usted le asegura que sus respuestas seran mantenidas en la mas completa confidencialidad y anonimidad. Dígale que sus respuestas son muy importantes para el éxito del estudio, y que incluso podrían resultar en proyectos gubernamentales o de otras agencias que beneficiarían la comunidad. Dígale que su participación es muy importante para que el estudio sea completo.

8. Después de terminar la entrevista, dígale que la encargada del estudio esta interesada en tomar algunas fotos de la comunidad donde se muestren actividades típicas de la familia. Pregúntele si podríamos incluirla.

9. Trate de mantener un flujo constante durante la entrevista, pero haga el esfuerzo de anotar la mayor cantidad posible de las respuestas y comentarios de las encuestadas. Puede escribir en los espacios provistos en el formulario, así como en los margenes.

10. Si una pregunta no coincide con la situación de la mujer encuestada, marque "N/A" ("no aplica") y siga adelante. Un ejemplo de ésto sería una pregunta sobre su marido siendo la entrevistada soltera.

Appendix B

Questionnaire, English Translation

AZUA REGION

PRINCIPAL RESEARCHER: B. FINLAY
DEPARTMENT OF SOCIOLOGY
TEXAS A&M UNIVERSITY
COLLEGE STATION, TEXAS 77843

SURVEYOR: GIVE THIS INTERVIEW TO THE <u>PRINCIPAL WOMAN</u> OF THE
HOUSE.   THAT IS, THE WOMAN WHO HAS THE MOST RESPONSIBILITY IN
THE HOME AND DOMESTIC TASKS, WHO IS THE HEAD OF THE HOUSE OR
THE WIFE OF THE HEAD.

Identification number of this survey: _____

Community: _____

Date: _____

Interviewer: _____

I. GENERAL CHARACTERISTICS AND DEMOGRAPHICS

1. Type of house

A. The predominant material of the house:

_____(1) reinforced concrete   _____(5) <u>yagua</u>,
<u>tejamani</u>

_____(2) wood   _____(6) scraps,
cartons,
_____(3) palm   <u>hojalata</u>,
etc.

_____(4) zinc   _____(7) other
(specify)

_____

B. Type of floor:

_____(1) mosaic, granite, or _____(3) wood
marble
_____(4) earth
_____(2) cement

C. Do you have electricity in your house?

_____ yes _____ no

D. Do you have running water inside?

_____ yes _____ no

2. Where were you born? _____

3. Did you spend most of your childhood in a rural or an urban area?

_____ rural _____ urban

4. Who did you live with most during your childhood?

_____(1) mother and father (with or without others)

_____(2) mother only

_____(3) father only

_____(4) mother and stepfather

_____(5) father and stepmother

_____(6) maternal grandparents, without parents

_____(7) paternal grandparents, without parents

_____(8) other, specify: _____

5. How many brothers and sisters do you have?

_____ brothers _____ sisters

6. Are your parents living?

_____(1) yes, both   Where do they live? _____

_____(2) mother only Where does she live? _____

_____(3) father only Where does he live? _____
(Go to question 8)

_____(4) No, neither (Go to question 8)

7. How often do you visit your mother?

_____(1) daily   _____(2) several times a week

_____(3) every week _____(4) several times a month

_____(5) every month _____(6) several times a year

_____(7) a year once or twice   _____(8) a year than once

8. At what age did you leave your parents' house?_____

9. Why did you leave? (to marry, to work, etc.)
   _____

   If work, where did you work and what did you do?
   _____

10. Where have you lived? (Mention the communities or
    places you lived for at least a month.)
    _____

11. How long have you lived in this community?
    _____ years   _____ months

II. COMPOSITION OF THE FAMILY AND OF THE HOUSEHOLD

12. Tell me, starting with yourself, the names of the
    family members of this household; that is, those who
    eat and sleep here the majority of the time. Tell me
    the first names only, and the other data that I will
    indicate.

NAME	SEX	AGE	RELATION TO YOU	MARITAL STATUS	HIGHEST GRADE PASSED	READ AND WRITE?
1.						
2.						
3.						
4. // 10.						

CODE: SEX: MARITAL STATUS: LITERATE:
        1-male   1-single   4-widowed   1-yes
        2-female   2-free union 5-divorced   2-no
                    3-married   6-separated

III. INCOME, RESOURCES, EXPENSES

13. Is this house rented, owned, or what?

_____(1) rented ____(2) owned ____(3) free ___ (4)other

14. How many <u>tareas</u> of land does this family have? _____

15. How much is in cultivation? _____ (if none, go to question 21)

16. Form of tenancy: _____(1) owned, with title_____ (2) owned, without title _____(3) rented _____ (4) borrowed _____(5) share-crop _____(6) other

17. What are your main crops?_____

18. Farm for _____(1) consumption _____(2) consumption and sale

_____(3) sale

19. Do you have livestock? _____(1) yes _____(2) no

Type   How Many?

20. Do you work on the family farm? _____(1) yes

_____(2) no

(If she says "yes" continue with a, b; If she says "no," go to question 21)

a. What work do you do? (the most important first)

_____

_____

b. How many days a month? _____

21. Does the family have any income in addition to your farm?

_____(1) yes _____(2) no (If "no," go to question 24)

22. Who in your family has an income and what do they
    do? (List each person, their activities, and
    monthly income during the past year)

PERSON	ACTIVITY (type of work)	WHOM DO THEY WORK FOR	MONTHLY INCOME	HOURS/ WEEK	MONTHS/ YEAR	STILL WORK THERE

(LIST ALL ACTIVITIES OF EACH PERSON.)

IF THE RESPONDENT WORKS FOR MONEY, ASK:

23. Who takes care of the children while you work?_____

24. Did you inherit your land from your father, from your
    mother, from both or others, or did you not inherit
    anything?

_____inherited from father

_____inherited from mother

_____inherited from both

_____inherited from others

_____did not inherit

What did you do with the
land you inherited?
(MARK MORE THAN ONE
ANSWER, IF NECESSARY)

_____still have all of it

_____sold part

_____sold all

_____gave part to husband
      or family

_____gave all to husband
      or family

_____has been taken, lost

_____other, specify:_____

25. Does this family receive help from:

_____ relatives in the country

_____ relatives from a foreign country

_____ pension or aid from the state government

26. What is the major source of income of the family?

_____(1) the land   _____(2) other activities

IF THE RESPONDENT IS NOT MARRIED OR IN A UNION, GO TO QUESTION 28.

27. What does your husband do with the income he makes? Does he give you enough for family necessities?

_____(1) yes _____(2) no

If no, why not? _____

28. Who decides what you spend on the family?

29. Who decides and who controls the money for the following purchases?

PURCHASE	DECIDES	CONTROLS	(Q. 30) EXPENSE
Food			
Clothes & Shoes			
Education			
Medicine			
House Repairs			
Work implements			
Livestock			
Household Goods			
Rent Payment			

30. For each of the purchases mentioned, how much did the family spend in the past year? (try to get an approximate amount) (READ THE PURCHASES AND NOTE THE EXPENSES.)

31. Did someone in the family borrow money last year?
_____ yes _____ no

Are all your debts paid?____(1) yes ____(2) no ____
(3) some

Who decides about borrowing money? _____

32. Who decides about the children's education? _____

33. Who keeps the family money?_____

IV. DISTRIBUTION OF HOUSEHOLD ACTIVITIES

Who does the following activities? (Mention the person who has
the greatest responsibility for the activity and others who
help that person.)

ACTIVITIES	PRINCIPAL (MAIN)	HELPERS
Preparation of food		
Taking care of and cleaning the house and the kitchen		
Taking care of clothes		
Taking care of the children		
Taking care of the birds		
Taking care of the animals		
Preparing the land (plowing)		
Planting		
Applying pesticides, herbicides, fertilizers		
Harvesting		
Sale of the farm products		

V. HEALTH AND NUTRITION

34. How many meals a day do the families of this community
eat? _____

35. How many meals a day does your family usually eat?

_____

36. If there is not enough for everyone, who eats more and who eats less? more: _____ less:_____

37. Of the listed foods, which ones does your family eat?

FOODS	FREQUENCY OF EATING				SOURCES		
	Daily	A few times a week	Occasionally	Never	Own Production	Purchase	Other
Milk							
Cheese							
Eggs							
Meat							
Fish/Seafood							
Fruits							
Salads (cabbage, tomato, etc.)							
Beans/Legumes							
Eggplant, Tayota							
Corn							
Rice							
Wheat							
Oatmeal							
Green Vegetables							
Plantains							
Tubers (yucca, yam, potato)							
Other (specify)							

38. How far is the nearest clinic? _____

39. How many times in the past year did you go to the clinic? _____ (You or another person in your family)

40. When your last baby was born, who attended the birth?
_____(1) doctor _____(2) midwife _____(3) specify other:

41. Where was this baby born? _____ (at home, hospital, etc.)

42. For how many months after the birth did you breast-feed the baby?_____

43. At what age (how many months) did you begin to give the baby other foods? _____

44. What other foods did you give the baby?

_____meat _____fruit _____vegetables _____eggs

_____milk _____other, specify_____

45. Have your children been vaccinated? ___(1)yes ___(2)no

46. How many illnesses were there in your family the past month?

	Illness	Duration (days)	What remedy was used?	Who was consulted?
ADULTS				
CHILDREN				

47. What preventive and curative medications do you use for the following types of illnesses?

ILLNESS	PREVENTIVE	CURATIVE
Respiratory (flu, cold, pneumonia)		
Gastrointestinal (diarrhea, stomach ache)		
Malnutrition (anemia, etc.)		

VI. MARITAL HISTORY AND FERTILITY

48. How many children have you had? _____

49. Are they all living now?_____ Yes (GO TO QUESTION 50)
    _____ No   How many died? _____

    At what age did they die and how did they die?

AGE	SEX	CAUSE OF DEATH

50. How old were you when your first child was born?
    _____ years

51. Did you have problems in pregnancy? (miscarriages, etc.)

52. At what age did you first get married (form a union)?

    _____ years   (IF RESPONDENT HAS NOT BEEN MARRIED/IN A UNION, GO TO QUESTION 58).

53. How many unions have you had? _____
    (IF ONE, GO TO QUESTION 56)

54. Have you been separated or divorced? ____ yes____ no
    How many times? _____
    After how much time together? _____ years
    (the last separation)
    Why did you separate? _____
    _____

55. Do you have children from a previous marriage?
_____ yes _____ no (GO TO QUESTION 56)

b. Does the father of these children give you anything
for them? _____ yes _____ no _____ not now, used to

c. How does he help you? _____

If you presently are married:

d. How do your present husband and the children of your
other marriage get along? _____

56. How long have you been married to your present husband?
_____ years

57. Do you believe that your present marriage is better or
worse than you expected (hoped for)?

_____(1) better
_____(2) worse
_____(3) neither better nor worse, but general
        satisfaction
_____(4) neither better nor worse, but some discontent
_____(5) other: _____

58. Generally, for a person in your situation, do you
believe that it is better to be married or simply to
live with a husband in free union?

_____(1) better married _____(2) better free union
_____(3) no difference, or I don't know, or it depends
Why? _____

_____

59. Do your children have godparents?
_____ yes _____ no _____ some of them

What do the godparents do for the children?

_____

60. How many children do you think is the ideal number for
a family? _____ Why this number? _____

_____

61. Do you expect to have more children? ____(1) yes
____(2) no _____(3) other, specify:_____

62. Generally, do you prefer sons or daughters?
_____ sons _____ daughters _____ no preference

Why? _____

63. Have you thought of using contraceptive methods so you do not have more children? _____(1) yes _____(2) no

b. Have you used any method?
_____ yes _____ no

c. What method did you use?   Why not? (GO TO
_____   QUESTION 64)

d. Do you still use it? _____ yes _____ no

Why not? _____
_____

64. Are you pregnant now?

_____(1) yes _____(2) no _____(3) don't know

65. Are there many women in the community who have had abortions?

_____(1) yes _____(2) no _____(3) don't know

Why do you think this is so?

VII. ATTITUDES ABOUT THE FAMILY AND THE ROLE OF WOMEN

66. In your opinion, what are the most important things a mother can teach her daughters?

67. What are the most important things to teach sons?

68. Please describe a good husband. What does he do, what characteristics does he have?

69. Are there many men like this? ____(1) yes _____(2) no

    If no, why?

70. What is the typical husband like in this community?

70b. Describe a good wife. What does she do, what characteristics does she have?

71. What do you think are the basic differences between men and women? And why do you think these differences exist?

VIII. ASPIRATIONS FOR YOUR CHILDREN

72. What do you want for your daughters? For example, how many years of school do you want your daughter to complete? _____ years

    b. At what age do you think your daughters should marry? _____

    c. What kind of job do you want your daughters to have?
       _____

    d. What kind of man do you want your daughters to marry?
       _____

    e. What other hopes do you have for your daughters?

       _____

       _____

73. What do you want for your sons?

    a. How many years of school do you want your sons to complete? _____ years

    b. What kind of job do you want your sons, to have?

    c. At what age do you think your sons should marry? _____ years

    d. What kind of woman do you want your sons to marry?

    _____

    e. What other hopes do you have for your sons?

    _____

IX. SOCIAL AND RELIGIOUS PARTICIPATION

74. Have you been baptized? _____(1) yes _____(2) no

75. Are you Catholic? _____(1) yes _____(2) no, specify:

_____

76. Is there a priest in this community? ____(1) yes ____(2) no

    Do you know him? _____(1) yes _____(2) no

    How often do you visit him? _____

77. How far away is the nearest church? _____

78. How frequently do you go to church to attend mass? ____ for other purposes? _____

    Codes: 1-at least once a month
           2-2 or 3 times a month
           3-once a month
           4-several times a year
           5-once a year
           6-never or rarely

79. And your husband, how frequently does he go to church to attend mass? _____ for other reasons? _____

80. Do you ever pray? _____(1) yes _____(2) no

    How frequently? _____(1) daily _____(2) several times
                 _____(3) less   a week

81. How far away is the children's school (primary level)?

_____

82. When do you rest? _____

83. When do you have fun or enjoy yourself? _____

_____

84. What do you do for enjoyment? _____

85. When does your husband have fun? _____

86. And what does he do to have fun? _____

87. Do you listen to the radio? _____(1) yes _____(2) no

    favorite program _____

88. How often do you go to the city or town? _____

89. Are there organizations in this community for women or
    the workers? _____(1) yes _____(2) no

    Do you participate in these organizations? _____

    Yes: Which organizations? _____

    No: Why not? _____

90. Did you vote in the elections last May? ____(1) yes
    ____(2) no

    Yes: How did you decide whom to vote for?_____
    _____

91. Are there persons who have left this home to go live in
    another community?_____ no _____ yes Please tell me
    more about them

Relation-ship to you	Sex	Age when left?	Age now?	Where do they live?	Why did they leave?	What kind of job do they have now?

92. Those who left, do they help or visit you? (How do they
    help you?)

93. Who is the person you feel closest to?

    NOTE THE RELATIONSHIP (for example, FRIEND, OLDEST
    DAUGHTER, HUSBAND, etc.)

Appendix C

Questionnaire, Spanish Version

ENCUESTA DE LA FAMILIA RURAL DOMINICANA

REGION DE AZUA

INVESTIGADORA PRINCIPAL: B. FINLAY
DEPARTMENT OF SOCIOLOGY
TEXAS A&M UNIVERSITY
COLLEGE STATION, TEXAS 77843

ENCUESTADORA; HAGA ESTA ENTREVISTA CON LA MUJER PRINCIPAL
DE LA CASA. ES DECIR, LA QUE TIENE LA MAYOR
RESPONSABILIDAD EN EL HOGAR Y LAS TAREAS DOMESTICAS, QUE
ES LA JEFA DE LA CASA O ESPOSA DEL JEFE.

Número de identificación de esta encuesta:_____

Comunidad:_____

Fecha:_____

Encuestadora:_____

I. CARACTERISTICAS GENERALES Y DEMOGRAFICAS

1. Tipo de casa   (ANOTE SIN PREGUNTAR, A Y B)

A. El material predominante en las paredes:

___1. concreto   ___5. yagua, tejamanil

___2. madera   ___6. deshechos, cartón,
                              hojalata, etc.
___3. palma   ___7. otra
                              (especifique):
___4. zinc   _____

B. Tipo de piso de la vivienda:

___1. mosaico, granito   ___3. madera
      o similares
___2. cemento   ___4. tierra

C. ¿Hay luz electrica en esta casa? ___sí ___no

D. ¿Tiene pluma o llave dentro de
   la casa (agua corriente)?   ___sí ___no

2. ¿Dónde nació usted?_____

3. ¿Pasó la mayoría de su infancia en la zona rural
   o urbana?   ___1. rural   ___2. urbana

4. ¿Con quién vivió durante la mayoría de su
   infancia?

___1. madre y padre (con otros o no)

___2. madre sola

___3. padre solo

___4. madre y padrastro

___5. padre y madrastra

___6. abuelos maternos, sin padres

___7. abuelos paternos, sin padres

___8. otro, especifique: _____

5. ¿Cuántos hermanos y hermanas tiene?
   ___hermanos   ___hermanas

6. ¿Viven sus padres?

___1. Sí, los dos .... ¿Dónde viven?_____
___2. Madre sola .... ¿Dónde vive ella?_____
___3. Padre solo .... ¿Dónde vive él?_____(PASE
                                           A P. 8)

7. ¿Con qué frecuencia ve a su madre?

___1. diario   ___5. como cada mes
___2. algunas veces por   ___6. algunas veces
      semana   por año
___3. cada semana   ___7. una o dos
                                      veces por año
___4. algunas veces por mes   ___8. menos de una
                                      vez por año

8. ¿A qué edad salió usted de la casa de sus padres?____ años

9. ¿Para qué salió? (para casarse, trabajar, etc.)___
   Si salió para trabajar,¿dónde trabajó y qué hizo?_____

10. ¿Dónde ha vivido usted? (mencione las comunidades o lugares en que vivió por lo menos un mes)_____

11. ¿Hace cuánto tiempo que vive en esta comunidad?
    _____años   _____meses

II. COMPOSICION FAMILIAR Y DEL HOGAR

12. Dígame, comenzando con usted, los nombres de los miembros de este hogar; es decir, los que comen y duermen aquí la mayor parte del tiempo. Dígame sus nombres sin apellidos, y los otros datos que voy a indicar:

NOMBRE	SEXO	EDAD	PARENTESCO O RELACION CON USTED	ESTADO CIVIL ACTUAL	ULTIMA CURSO QUE APROBO	SABE LEER Y ESCRIBIR
1.						
2.						
3.						
4.						
5.						
6.						
7.						
8.						
9.						
10.						

III.   INGRESOS, RECURSOS, Y GASTOS

13. ¿Esta casa está alquilada, es propia, o qué?

___1. alquilada   ___3. cedida gratis

___2. propia   ___4. otro

14. ¿Cuántas tareas de tierra tiene esta familia?_____

15. ¿Cuánta tierra cultiva?_____(SI NINGUNA, PASE A
                                              P. 21)

16. Forma de tenencia:

___1. propia con título   ___4. prestada

___2. propia sin título   ___5. aparcería

___3. arrendada   ___6. otro

17. ¿Cuáles son los cultivos principales?_____

18. Cultivo para:

___1. consumo   ___3. venta

___2. consumo y venta

19. ¿Tiene ganado?   ___1. sí   ___2. no

Tipo:_____ ¿Cuántos tiene?_____

20. ¿Trabaja usted en el predio (parcela agrícola) de
la familia?   ___1. sí   ___2. no

(SI ELLA DICE "SI" SIGUE CON a, b; SI DICE "NO"
PASE A P. 21)

a. ¿Qué labores hace? (lo más importante primero)
b. ¿Cuántos días al mes?

21. ¿Tiene su familia ingresos fuera de su finca
(parcela)?   ___1. sí   ___2. no

(SI "NO" PASE A P. 24)

22. ¿Quiénes en su familia tienen ingresos y qué
hacen? (Liste cada persona, sus actividades, y
sus ingresos mensuales durante este último año.)

PER-SONA	ACTIVI-DADES	PARA QUIEN TRA-BAJA	INGRESOS MENSUALES	CUANTAS HORAS POR SEMANA	CUANTOS MESES POR ANO	TRABAJA AHI TODAVIA
-----	--------	------	----------	--------	-------	-------
-----	--------	------	----------	--------	-------	-------
-----	--------	------	----------	--------	-------	-------
-----	--------	------	----------	--------	-------	-------
-----	--------	------	----------	--------	-------	-------
-----	--------	------	----------	--------	-------	-------
-----	--------	------	----------	--------	-------	-------
-----	--------	------	----------	--------	-------	-------

(LISTE TODAS LAS ACTIVIDADES DE CADA PERSONA)

SI LA ENCUESTADA TRABAJA POR DINERO, PREGUNTELE:

23. ¿Quién cuida los niños mientras usted trabaja?____

24. ¿Heredó usted tierra de su padre, de su madre, de
los dos o otros, o no heredó?

____1. heredó de su padre
____2. heredó de su madre
____3. heredó de los dos
____4. heredó de otros
____5. no heredó

¿Qué hizo con la tierra que heredó?
(MARQUE MAS DE UNA RESPUESTA, SI ES NECESARIO)

____1. la conserva toda
____2. vendió una parte
____3. vendió todo
____4. cedérsela parcialmente a su marido
       o familiares
____5. cedérsela totalmente a su marido o
       familiares
____6. se la quitaron
____7. otro, especifique:_____

25. ¿Esta familia recibe ayuda de:

    ____1. familiares residentes en el país?
    ____2. familiares residentes en el extranjero?
    ____3. pensiones o ayudas del Estado?

26. ¿Cuál es la mayor fuente de ingresos de la familia?
    ____1. la parcela   ____2. las otras actividades

SI NO ESTA ACTUALMENTE CASADA O EN UNION, PASE A P. 28

27. ¿Qué hace su marido con los ingresos que él gana?_____

    ¿Le da suficiente para las necesidades de la familia?   ____1. sí   ____2. no
    Si no, ¿porque "no"?

28. ¿Quién decide en qué va a gastar dinero en su familia?_____

29. ¿Quién decide y quién controla el dinero para las siguientes compras?

COMPRAS	DECIDE	CONTROLA	GASTOS
Alimentos			
Ropa y calzado			
Educación			
Medicinas			
Reparaciones de la casa			
Implementos de trabajo			
Ganados			
Enseres domésticos			
Pagar la renta			

30. Para cada una de las compras que mencione, ¿cuánto gastó la familia el año pasado? (Trate de conseguir la cantidad aproximada)
(LEA LAS COMPRAS Y ANOTE LOS GASTOS)

31. ¿Alguien en la familia tomó prestados el año
    pasado? ___1. sí ___2. no

    ¿Están pagadas sus deudas?
    ___1. sí ___2. no ___3. algunas

    ¿Quién toma la decisión de tomar prestado?_____

32. ¿Quién decide sobre la educación de los niños?____

33. ¿Quién guarda el dinero de la familia?_____

IV. DISTRIBUCION DE ACTIVIDADES DEL HOGAR

    ¿Quiénes hacen las siguientes actividades?
    (Mencione la persona que tiene la mayor
    responsabilidad para la actividad, y otras
    quienes le ayudan.)

ACTIVIDADES	PRINCIPAL(ES)	AYUDANTES
preparación de alimentos		
cuidado y limpieza de la casa y de la cocina		
cuidado de ropa		
cuidado de los niños		
cría de aves		
cría de animales		
preparación de la tierra para agricultura		
siembra		
aplicación de las pesticidas herbicidas, fertilizantes		
cosecha		
venta de los productos de la finca		

V. SALUD Y NUTRICION

34. ¿Cuántas comidas al día hacen las familias en esta comunidad?_____

35. ¿Cuántas comidas al día acostumbra a hacer su familia?_____

36. Si no hay suficiente para todos, ¿quién come más y quién come menos? más:_____ menos:_____

37. De los alimentos enumerados, ¿cuáles consume la familia?

ALIMENTOS	FRECUENCIA DE COMER					FUENTES	
	A diario	una vez por semana	ocasionalmente	nunca	producción propia	compra	otra
leche							
queso							
huevos							
carnes							
pes/ mariscos							
frutas							
ensaladas							
frijoles/ guandules							
beren- jenas							
maíz							
arroz							
trigo							
avena							
verduras							
platanos							
tubercu- los							

38. ¿A qué distancia se encuentra la clínica más
    cerca?_____

39. ¿Cuántas veces, el año pasado, fue a la clínica?
    (usted o otra persona en su familia)_____

40. Cuando nació su último bebé, ¿quién le ayudó?

    ___1. médico

    ___2. comadrona

    ___3. otro, especifique:_____

41. ¿Dónde nació este bebé?_____
    (en casa, hospital, etc.)

42. ¿Hasta cuántos meses después del parto le da el
    pecho al niño?_____

43. ¿A cuántos meses comienza a darle otros alimentos?
    _____

44. Mencione los alimentos que adiciona a la
    alimentación del lactante:

    ___carnes   ___frutas   ___legumbres   ___huevos

    ___leche   ___otros, especifique:_____

45. ¿Ha vacunado a sus hijos? ___1. sí   ___2. no

46. ¿Cuántos enfermos hubo en su familia el mes
    pasado?

	Enfermedad	Duración	¿Qué remedio usó?	¿A quién consultó?
ADULTOS:				
NINOS:				

47. ¿Qué medidas preventivas y curativas usa?

ENFERMEDAD	PREVENTIVAS	CURATIVAS
Respiratorias (gripe, catarro, pulmonía)		
Gastro-intestinales (diarrea, dolor de vientre)		
Desnutrición (anemia, etc.)		

VI. HISTORIA MARITAL Y LA FERTILIDAD

48. ¿Cuántos niños ha tenido?_____

49. ¿Viven todos ahora? ___1. sí (PASE A P. 50)
___2. no

¿Cuántos se murieron?_____

¿A qué edad se murieron su(s) niño(s), y qué causó la muerte?

EDAD	SEXO	CAUSA DE LA MUERTE

50. ¿Qué edad tenía usted cuando nació su primer niño? _____años

51. ¿Tuvo algún problema en el embarazo? (abortos, etc.) ___1. sí   ___2. no

52. ¿A qué edad se unió por primera vez (con marido)? _____años

SI NO HA TENIDO NINGUNA UNION, PASE A P. 58

53. ¿Cuántas uniones ha tenido? ____ (SI UNA, PASE A P. 56)

54. ¿Estado separada o divorciada? ___1. sí   ___2. no

    ¿Cuántas veces?_____

    ¿Después de cuánto tiempo juntos?____años   (la
    última separación)

    ¿Por qué se separaron?

55. ¿Tiene niños de otra unión previa?
    ___1. sí   ___2. no (PASE A P. 56)

    (b) ¿El padre de estos niños le da a usted algo
        para ellos?   ___1. sí   ___2. no

                      ___3. ahora no, antes, sí

    (c) ¿Cómo él le ayuda?_____

    (SI ESTA ACTUALMENTE EN UNION):
    (d) ¿Cómo se lleva con su marido actual y los
        niños de la otra unión?_____

56. ¿Hace cuánto tiempo que se unió con su marido
    actual? ____años

57. ¿Cree que esta unión actual es mejor o peor de lo
    que esperaba?

    ___1. mejor

    ___2. peor

    ___3. ni mejor ni peor, pero expreso satisfacción
         general

    ___4. ni mejor ni peor, pero expreso algún
         descontenta

    ___5. otra:_____

58. Generalmente, para una persona en su situación,
    ¿cree que es mejor casarse o simplemente vivir
    con marido en unión libre?

    ___1. mejor casarse

    ___2. mejor la unión libre

    ___3. no hay diferencia, o no sé, o depende
         ¿Por qué?_____

59. ¿Tiene padrinos sus niños?
___1. sí ___2. no ___3. algunos

¿Qué hacen los padrinos por los niños?_____

60. ¿Cuántos niños piensa usted son el número ideal
para una familia?____ ¿Por qué este número?_____

61. ¿Espera usted tener más hijos?
___1. sí ___2. no ___3. otro, especifique:___

62. Generalmente, ¿prefiere hijos o hijas?
___1. hijos ___2. hijas

___3. ni hijos ni hijas

¿Por qué?_____

63. ¿Ha pensado en usar los métodos contraceptivos
para no tener más hijos? ___1. sí ___2. no

(b) ¿Ha usado algún método?
___1. sí ___2. no ¿Por qué no?_____
(PASE A P. 64)

(c) ¿Cuál método usó?_____

(d) ¿Todavía lo usa?
___1. sí ___2. no ¿Por qué no?_____

64. ¿Ahora está encinta?
___1. sí ___2. no ___3. no sé

65. ¿Hay muchas mujeres en esta comunidad que han
tenido abortos? ___1. sí ___2. no ___3. no sé

¿Qué piensa de éso?_____

VII. ACTITUDES SOBRE LA FAMILIA Y EL PAPEL DE MUJER

66. En su opinión, ¿cuáles son las cosas más
importantes que una madre puede ensenar a sus
hijas?_____

67. ¿Cuáles son las cosas más importantes a ensenar a
los hijos?

68. Por favor, describa un buen marido. ¿Qué hace,
cuáles características tiene?_____

69. ¿Son muchos los hombres así? ___1. sí ___2. no
Si "no": ¿Por qué?_____

70. ¿Cómo es el marido típico en esta comunidad?

(b) Describe una buena esposa o mujer. ¿Qué hace, cuáles características tiene?_____

71. ¿Cuáles, piensa usted, son las diferencias básicas entre los hombres y las mujeres y por qué existen las diferencias?_____

VIII. ASPIRACIONES PARA LOS HIJOS

72. ¿Qué quiere para sus hijas? Por ejemplo, ¿cuántos años de educación quiere que ellas completen? ___años

(b) ¿A qué edad piensa que ellas deben casarse?__

(c) ¿Qué tipo de ocupación quiere que ellas tengan?_____

(d) ¿Qué tipo de esposo desea para ellas?_____

(e) ¿Cuáles otras aspiraciones tiene para sus hijas?_____

73. ¿Qué quiere para sus hijos?

(a) ¿Cuántos años de educación quiere que ellos completen?_____

(b) ¿Qué tipo de ocupación quiere que ellos tengan?_____

(c) ¿A qué edad piensa que deben casarse?_____

(d) ¿Qué tipo de esposa desea para ellos?_____

(e) ¿Cuáles otras aspiraciones tiene para sus hijos?_____

IX. PARTICIPACION SOCIAL Y RELIGIOSA

74. ¿Está usted bautizada? ___1. sí ___2. no

75. ¿Es católica? ___1. sí ___2. no, especifique:___

76. ¿Hay un sacerdote para esta comunidad?
___1. sí   ___2. no

¿Usted lo conoce? ___1. sí   ___2. no

¿Con qué frecuencia usted lo visita?_____

77. ¿A qué distancia se encuentra la iglesia más cerca?_____

78. ¿Con qué frecuencia va a la iglesia para oir misa?_____   ¿Para otros propósitos?_____

CODIGOS: 1. por lo menos una vez por semana
          2. 2-3 veces por mes
          3. como una vez por mes
          4. unas veces por año
          5. una vez por año
          6. nunca o raramente

79. Y su marido, ¿con qué frecuencia él va a la iglesia para oir misa?____   ¿Para otros propósitos?____

80. ¿Alguna vez reza? ___1. sí   ___2. no

¿Con qué frecuencia?
___1. diariamente

___2. unas veces por semana

___3. menos, como:_____

81. ¿A qué distancia se encuentra la escuela para los niños (al nivel primario)?_____

82. ¿Cuándo descansa usted?_____

83. ¿Cuándo se divierte usted?_____

84. ¿Qué hace para divertirse?_____

85. ¿Cuándo se divierte su marido?_____

86. ¿Y qué hace él para divertirse?_____

87. ¿Escucha radio? ___1. sí Programa preferido:_____
                     ___2. no

88. ¿Cada cuánto tiempo va al pueblo o ciudad?_____

89. ¿Hay organizaciones en esta comunidad para las
    mujeres o los trabajadores? ___1. sí   ___2. no

    ¿Participa usted en estas organizaciones?
    ___1. sí ¿Cuáles organizaciones?_____
    ___2. no ¿Por qué no?_____

90. ¿Votó usted en las elecciones el mayo pasado?
    ___1. sí ¿Cómo decidió por quien votar?_____
    ___2. no

91. ¿Hay personas que han salido de este hogar para
    irse a vivir fuera de la comunidad?
    ___1. no
    ___2. sí Dígame, por favor, más de ellos.

¿Cuál es el parentesco con usted?	Sexo	¿Qué edad tenía cuando salió?	¿Qué edad tiene ahora?	¿Dónde vive?	¿Por qué salió?	¿Qué tipo de trabajo tiene ahora?

92. Los que salieron, ¿le ayudan o visitan?_____
    (¿Cómo le ayudan?)_____

93. ¿Cuál es la persona con quien se siente más cerca?
    (más identificación emocional)_____
    ANOTE SU RELACION (por ejemplo, AMIGA, HIJA
    MAYOR, MARIDO, ETC.)

References

Abraham-Van der Mark, Eva E. 1983. The impact of industrialization on women: A Caribbean case. In June Nash and Maria P. Fernandez-Kelly, eds., *Women, men, and the international division of labor*, Ch. 15. Albany: State University of New York Press.

Alvarez, Fausto B. 1988. *The effect of sociocultural factors on the quality of relations of the United States with Hispaniola: Analysis of the American military occupation of Haiti and the Dominican Republic (1915-1934)*. Unpublished master's thesis, Department of Sociology, Texas A&M University, College Station, Texas.

Arango, Amparo. 1985. *La division del trabajo por sexo en la zona rural*. Paper presented at Seminario Diagnostico sobre la Mujer Rural Dominicana, December 11-12, 1985. Sponsored by Centro de Investigation para la Accion Femenina (CIPAF), Santo Domingo.

Arizpe, Lourdes, and Josefina Aranda. 1981. The "comparative advantages" of women's disadvantages: Women workers in the strawberry export agribusiness in Mexico. *Signs* 7:453-473.

Baez, Clara. 1986. *La subordinacion de la mujer dominicana en cifras*. Santo Domingo: INSTRAW.

Bane, Mary Jo. 1976. *Here to stay: The American family in the twentieth century.* New York: Harper & Row.

Bell, Ian. 1981. *The Dominican Republic.* Boulder, CO: Westview.

Blood, R. O., and D. M. Wolfe. 1960. *Husbands and wives: The dynamics of married living.* New York: Free Press.

Boserup, Ester. 1970. *Women's role in economic development.* New York: St. Martin's Press.

Brown, Susan E. 1975. Love unites them and hunger separates them: Poor women in the Dominican Republic. In Rayna R. Reiter, ed., *Toward an anthropology of women.* New York: Monthly Review Press.

Cebotarev, Eleanora. 1979. *Mujer rural y desarrollo.* Ottawa: International Development Research Center.

Censo nacional de poblacion y vivienda. 1981. Santo Domingo: Oficina Nacional de Estadisticas.

Cross-Beras, Julio A. 1980. The Dominican family. In Man Singh Das and Clinton J. Jesser, eds., *The family in Latin America.* New Delhi: Vikas.

Curtin, Leslie B. 1982. *Status of women: A comparative analysis of twenty developing countries.* Reports on the World Fertility Survey. Washington, DC: Population Reference Bureau.

DeLaine, Bernard. 1987. *Projecto manejo de aguas nivel de finca (On-farm management project),* USAID Project no. 517-0159. Informe Final. Unpublished.

El Sol. 1987. Sin melones: Virosis destruye cosecha en Azua: Agroquimico esteriliza suelo. Santo Domingo, February 2, pp. 1, 3.

Enciclopedia dominicana. 1978. 2nd ed., Vol. 1. Santo Domingo: Enciclopedia Dominicana, S.A.

Feinberg, Richard E. 1984. *Report of the Atlantic Council's Working Group on the Caribbean Basin.* Boston: Oegeschlager, Gunn and Hain.

Fernandez-Kelly, Maria P. 1983. *For we are sold, I and my people: Women and industry in Mexico's frontier.* Albany: State University of New York Press.

Fiske, Amos K. 1899. *The West Indies: A history of the islands of the West Indian archipelago, together with an account of their physical characteristics, natural resources, and present conditions.* New York: Putnam.

Flora, Cornelia B., and Blas Santos. 1986. Women in family systems in Latin America. In June Nash, Helen I. Safa, and Contributors, *Women and change in Latin America.* South Hadley, MA: Bergin & Garvey.

Fortmann, Louise, and Dianne Rocheleau. 1984. Why agroforestry needs women: Four myths and a case study. *Unasylva* 36(4):2-11.

Froebel, Folker, Jurgen Heinrichs, and Otto Kreye. 1978. Export-oriented industrialization of underdeveloped countries. *Monthly Review* 30(6):22-27.

Geggus, David P. 1982. *Slavery, war, and revolution: The British occupation of Saint-Domingue, 1793-1798.* Oxford: Clarendon Press.

Gleijeses, Piero. 1978. *The Dominican crisis: The 1965 constitutionalist revolt and American intervention.* Baltimore: Johns Hopkins University Press.

Heinl, Robert D., and Nancy G. Heinl. 1978. *Written in blood: The story of the Haitian people, 1492-1971.* Boston: Houghton Mifflin.

Knight, Melvin M. 1970. *The Americans in Santo Domingo.* New York: Arno Press.

Lappé, Frances M., and Joseph P. Collins. 1979. *Food first: Beyond the myth of scarcity.* New York: Ballentine Books.

Leacock, Eleanor, Helen I. Safa, and Contributors. 1986. *Women's work: Development and the division of labor by gender.* South Hadley, MA: Bergin & Garvey.

Lenski, Gerhard. 1966. *Power and privilege: A theory of social stratification.* New York: McGraw-Hill.

Leyburn, James G. 1966 (1941). *The Haitian people*. New Haven: Yale University Press.

Lim, Linda Y. C. 1983. Capitalism, imperialism, and patriarchy: The dilemma of third-world women workers in multi-national factories. In June Nash and Maria P. Fernandez-Kelly, eds., *Women, men, and the international division of labor*, Ch. 3. Albany: State University of New York Press.

Lowenthal, Abraham F. 1972. *The Dominican intervention*. Cambridge, MA: Harvard University Press.

Massiah, Joycelin. 1983. *Women as heads of households in the Caribbean*. Colchester, Essex: UNESCO.

Morgan, Robin, ed. 1984. *Sisterhood is global: The international women's movement anthology*. New York: Anchor/Doubleday.

Moses, Yolanda T. 1977. Female status, the family, and male dominance in a West Indian community. In Wellesley Editorial Committee, *Women and national development: The complexities of change*, pp. 142-153. Chicago: University of Chicago Press.

MUDE (Mujeres en Desarrollo Dominicana). 1985. *Mujer rural hoy y mañana*. Santo Domingo: Mujeres en Desarrollo Dominicana, Inc.

Nash, June, and Maria P. Fernandez-Kelly, eds. 1983. *Women, men, and the new international division of labor*. Albany: State University of New York Press.

Nash, June, and Helen Safa, eds. 1986. *Women and change in Latin America*. South Hadley, MA: Bergin & Garvey.

ONE (Oficina Nacional de Estadisticas). 1980. *ONAPLAN. Encuesta nacional rural de mano de obra*, octubre, 1980. Santo Domingo: ONE.

Paxton, John, ed. 1987. *The statesman's yearbook*, 124th ed., 1987-88. London: Macmillan.

Retherford, R. D. 1975. *The changing sex differentials in*

mortality. Westport, CT: Greenwood Press.

Safa, Helen I. 1986. Runaway shops and female employment: The search for cheap labor. In Eleanor Leacock, H. Safa, and Contributors, *Women's work: Development and the division of labor by gender*, pp. 58-71. South Hadley, MA: Bergin & Garvey.

Tancer, Shoshana B. 1973. La Quisqueyana: The Dominican woman, 1940-1970. In Ann Pescatello ed., *Female and male in Latin America*, pp. 209-229. Pittsburgh: University of Pittsburgh Press.

Theodorson, George. 1965. Romanticism and motivation to marry in the United States, Singapore, Burma, and India. *Social Forces* 44(September): 17-27.

Tiano, Susan. 1987. Gender, work, and world capitalism: Third World women's role in development. In Beth B. Hess and Myra M. Ferree, eds., *Analyzing gender: A handbook of social science*, pp. 216-243. New York: Sage.

USAID (U.S. Agency for International Development). 1982. *Women in Development*. AID Policy Paper. Washington, DC: US Government Printing Office.

Weddle, Ken. 1974. *Haiti in pictures*. New York: Sterling Publishing Company.

Weeks, John R. 1986. *Population: An introduction to concepts and issues*, 3rd ed. Belmont, CA: Wadsworth.

Weil, Thomas E. 1973. *Area handbook for the Dominican Republic*, 2nd ed. Washington, DC: U.S. Government Printing Office.

Wiarda, Howard, and Michael J. Kryzanek. 1982. *The Dominican Republic: A Caribbean crucible*. Boulder, CO: Westview.

Index

About the Author

BARBARA FINLAY is an Associate Professor of Sociology at Texas A&M University, where she has taught since 1982. Her interest in the family and rural women goes back to her graduate student days at the University of Florida. Her Ph.D. dissertation at that institution was on the history of rural black families in Florida. She has published two books and a number of articles, mostly in the fields of research methods, the sociology of the family, and gender issues. Her current research interests continue to be in the field of women and development, with a focus on the Caribbean area.